THE COMPLETE BOOK
of
HARDANGER

THE COMPLETE BOOK

of

HARDANGER

JANNY GELDENS

Dedication

This book is dedicated to my granddaughter Danica. It would never have been written if it were not for the repeated requests and encouragement of my friends and students. For a long time it was "why are you not writing a book?". Then it became "when are you going to write a book?". After more encouragement from friends and students, my dear friend Judy Baker touched a soft spot and said, "You owe it to Danica". That gave me the inspiration I needed.

I hope this book gives everyone interested in this wonderful technique as much pleasure as it has given me in writing it.

Acknowledgements

To have Peggy, Muriel and Judy as friends is invaluable. Their encouragement and support, and the unstinting time they gave me throughout the writing of this book is greatly appreciated.

My thanks go to my students who so often encouraged and contributed so much by their constant queries.

My sincere thanks to Mitzi who so expertly did all the photography. Her sense of colour, perfection and patience, made this book in true colours.

Last, but not least, my gratitude to Shelley who so skilfully typed all my notes.

Janny Geldens

Contents

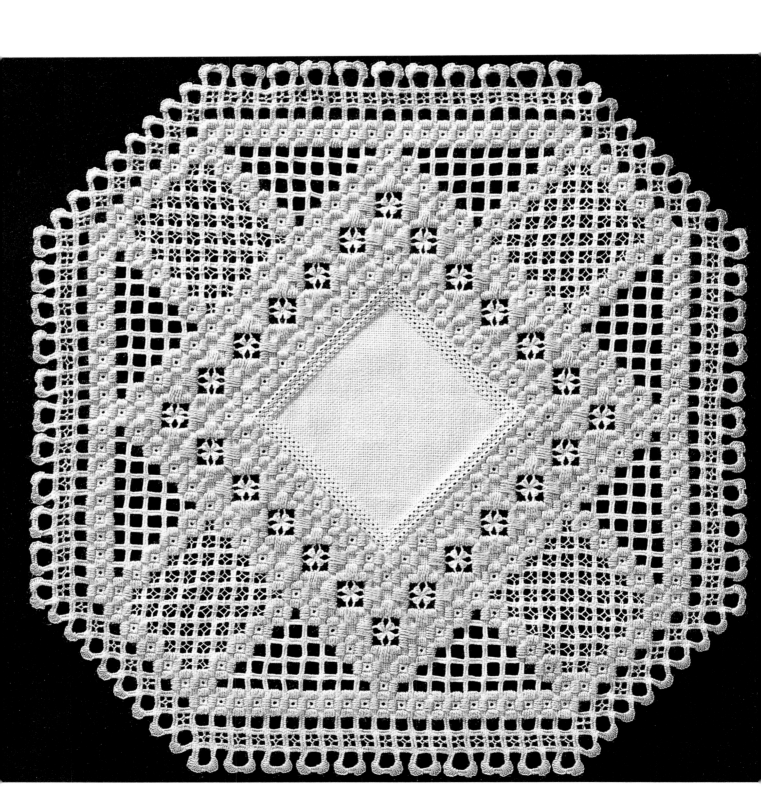

Introduction

The craft of Hardanger is thought to have originated in Persia and travelled via Asia to become a traditional embroidery in Norway. The name comes from the small town of Hardanger on the Fjord of the same name on the west coast of Norway.

The Norwegian national costume, which varies from region to region, is called *Bunad* and it is worn at official and festive occasions. *Bunader* (plural of Bunad) are composed of several garments worn together to form the total costume. It is important for each detail to be correct, even to the stockings and shoes. (See photograph on page below).

In this book I have provided graphs for basic Hardanger designs, with written explanations, followed by more advanced projects. Finally there is a gallery of my completed works to show applications of the craft.

MATERIALS

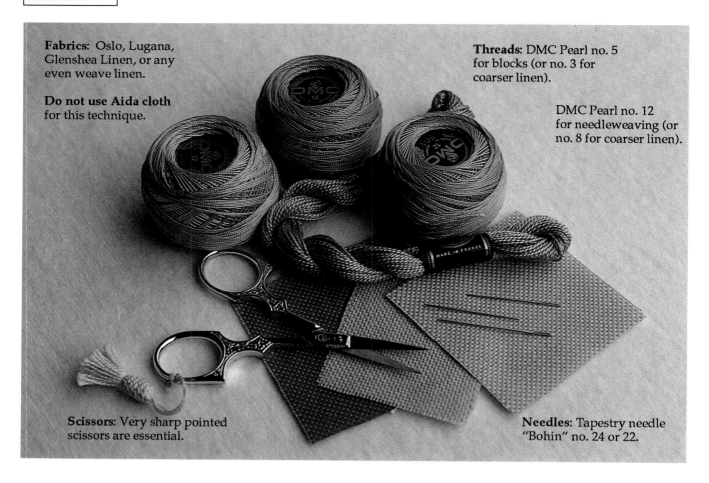

Fabrics: Oslo, Lugana, Glenshea Linen, or any even weave linen.

Do not use Aida cloth for this technique.

Threads: DMC Pearl no. 5 for blocks (or no. 3 for coarser linen).

DMC Pearl no. 12 for needleweaving (or no. 8 for coarser linen).

Scissors: Very sharp pointed scissors are essential.

Needles: Tapestry needle "Bohin" no. 24 or 22.

ABBREVIATIONS
FT = fabric thread
SS = satin stitch
BHS = buttonhole stitch

How to keep the Twist in your Thread

How to finish a Thread

How to thread your Needle
Note short tail

CHAPTER ONE

Kloster Blocks

KLOSTER = satin stitch
KLOSTER BLOCK = 5 stitches over four threads

Variations of these blocks are illustrated on the next pages. When starting a project, overcast the edges of your fabric. All kloster blocks are embroidered before threads are cut and removed.

Two ways of cutting threads are illustrated in Graphs A and B. The green lines and the numeral 4 on both Graphs indicate the threads to be cut and removed.

The remaining threads are called **bars**. These can be needlewoven in many different ways. Most important is the correct counting of threads **not** holes. As all diamond or square shapes of blocks are opposite each other, it is essential to use a perfect even weave fabric.

All blocks are made in a diagonal fashion, and the needleweaving is done in the same way. The reason for this is because of the principle on which Hardanger is based. When blocks are embroidered, threads cut and removed, the remaining space will be a perfect square. When following a graph, make sure that the vertical block is opposite the vertical, and that the horizontal block is opposite the horizontal.

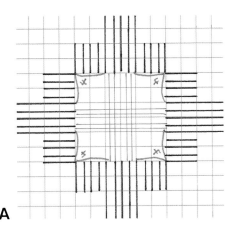

A

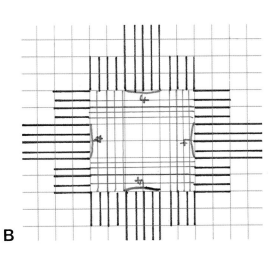

B

The Basic Stitches

LESSON ONE

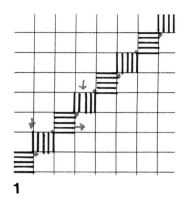

1

1

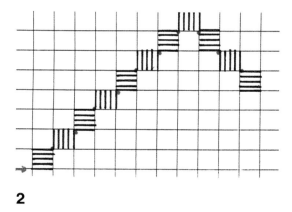

2

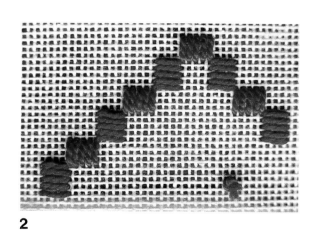

2

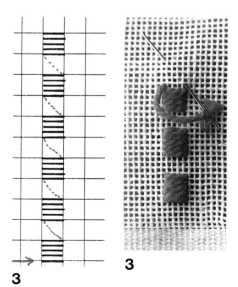

3

3

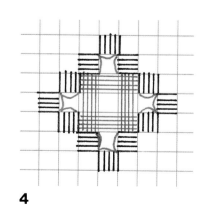

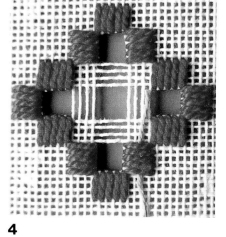

4

4

Graph 1 and Sample 1

Begin at the arrow, and leave a waste knot on top of the fabric. (This thread will be finished off later). *Work 5 SS over 4 FT. Move the needle up 4 FT then insert it in the same hole as the last stitch of the first block. Work 5 SS over 4 FT. Bring the needle up in the same hole as the last stitch and take it 4 FT to the right to start the next block*. Continue the sequence. There are now vertical and horizontal blocks in a diagonal fashion.

Note. Make sure that the last and first stitch of each block enter the same hole. This applies throughout the work. The red dot on the graph indicates where the threads meet.

Graph 2 and Sample 2

Follow instructions in Graph 1 from * to *. Then turn the corner, always with the vertical block on top. Now you can check whether the blocks are correct by running a ruler or your needle across from block to block.

 Always check that the blocks are in alternate horizontal and vertical directions.

Graph 3 and Sample 3

Blocks worked in a straight line showing how the thread is diagonally carried from block to block.

Graph 4 and Sample 4

Completed diamond of 4 blocks each way. The red lines on the graph represent the threads left after four threads have been cut and removed, as indicated by the green markings. Sample 4 shows the result. The yellow thread indicates that these threads must **never** be cut because on that side the stitches do not cover the fabric.

Graph 5 and Sample 5

A larger block in the diamond shape. The green markings and arrows on the graph show where to cut the threads. The red lines are the remaining threads. See Sample 5.

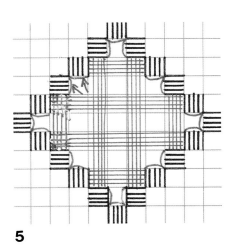

5

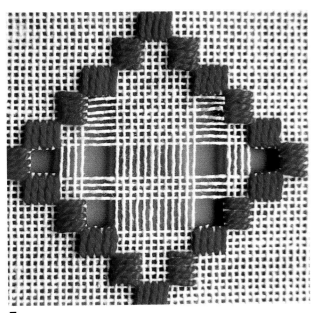

5

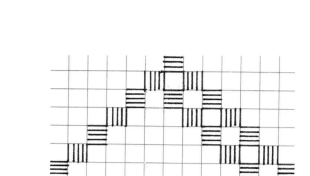

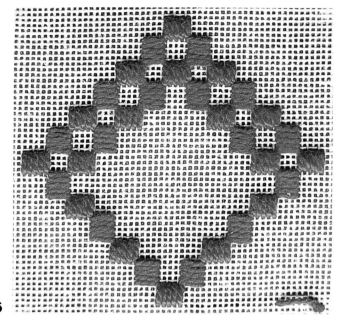

6

6

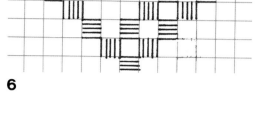

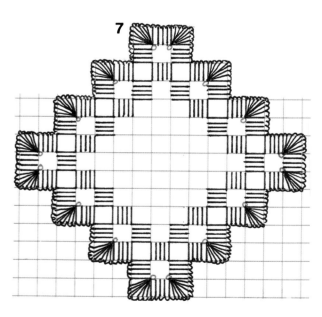

7

7

Graph 6 and Sample 6

A double row of blocks clearly shows the horizontal matching the horizontal blocks, and the vertical matching the vertical blocks.

Graph 7 and Sample 7

The traditional way of finishing Hardanger is with a buttonhole edge. Following the line of the previous block of SS, commence by inserting the needle four threads above the first stitch of the top block (see graph and sample). Work 5 BHS, move along top and work 4 BHS, each returning to the same hole as the last BHS just made. Turn corner and, moving four threads along, work BHS still returning to the same hole. There are now nine BHS in the same hole.

Move along next four threads, work four more BHS, completing the corner.

Note: The last BHS enters the same hole as the last five SS of the previous block.

Sample A shows how to start the next button-hole corner. Sample B shows where to insert the needle when thread runs out and where to begin the new thread. Pull old thread and finish off at back of the work. Continue with the new thread.

It is necessary to cover all threads around the corners, as the fabric is cut away when the project is finished. Uncovered threads may escape, weakening the work.

Graph 8 and Sample 8

Outside blocks are as described in Graph 1. The green block inside the first row of blocks is worked as follows:

4 SS over 4 FT; 5 SS over 8 FT; 4 SS over 4 FT. As shown before, all blocks are worked in a diagonal fashion. The larger blocks are worked in the same way. One block has been completed to show the result.

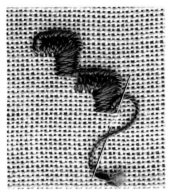

7A

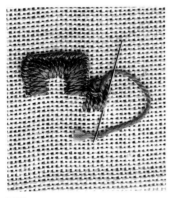

7B

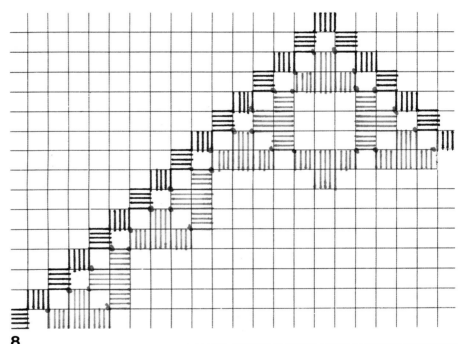

8

8

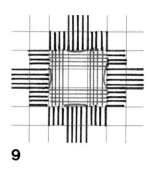

9

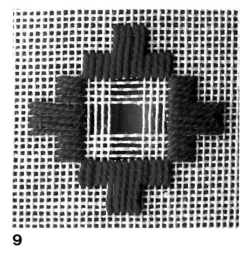

9

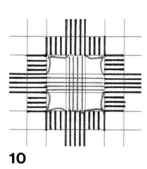

10

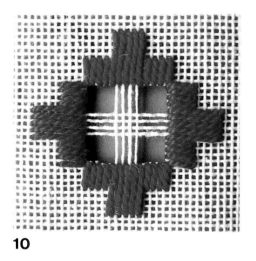

10

Graph 9 and Sample 9

A large block as described in Graph 8, with 4 FT cut and removed from the centre, as indicated by the green markings. The red lines show remaining threads.

Graph 10 and Sample 10

A large block as described in Graph 8, with 4 FT cut and removed as indicated by the green markings. The red lines are the remaining threads.

Graph 11 and Sample 11

Square blocks with eyelets. Note that the vertical and horizontal blocks are opposite each other. Sample 11 shows the eyelet with yellow thread, starting from corner to centre. Continue every thread to centre all around. Always pull the thread away from the centre, not straight up or away from the block.

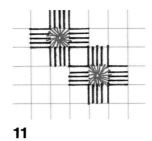

11

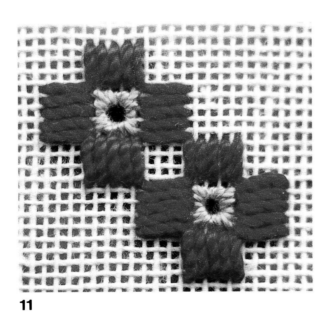

11

DO'S AND DON'TS

Do not leave loose threads at the back of the work. Start and finish each thread as illustrated in Chapter One, Lesson One.

Never cut and remove threads on both sides of a single block. Only four threads will remain and the fabric will be weak.

Do not forget that the **last** and **first** SS joins the same hole of your fabric. See Chapter 1, Graph 1 and Graph 8 - indicated by red dots.

Do count the threads to be cut carefully before you snip.

If you have cut one thread too many, take one thread from the edge of the fabric and weave it carefully into the space of the cut thread.

Fabric threads must never be distorted or holes created by working the satin stitches too tightly.

Do not have **holes** on either side of a Kloster block.

Do not have **holes** on the side of the Kloster block when making eyelets.

Do not leave **whiskers** after cutting threads right up to the Kloster block.

CHAPTER TWO

Needleweaving

Each of the thirty Kloster Blocks used in this chapter is worked as follows:
4 SS over 4 FT
5 SS over 8 FT
4 SS over 4 FT.
Form into a square.

A different method of needleweaving is shown on each block, and all needleweaving is worked with No. 12 Pearl thread.

Sampler 2 has been worked with a different design of buttonhole stitch for the edging on each side.

Graph 1 and Samples 1a and 1b

The threads are cut and removed as in Graph A. Bring the needle up between the 4 threads of the bar and weave over and under the 2 threads eight times on either side. Then take the needle diagonally to the next bar, as indicated by the arrow, and come up at the red dot. Weave this bar. Then take the thread to the back of the block and to the centre of the next bar. Needleweave this bar, then take the needle diagonally to the next bar. Finish the thread at the back of the block.

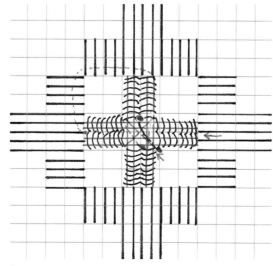

1

SAMPLER TWO

1

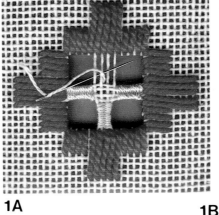

1A

1B

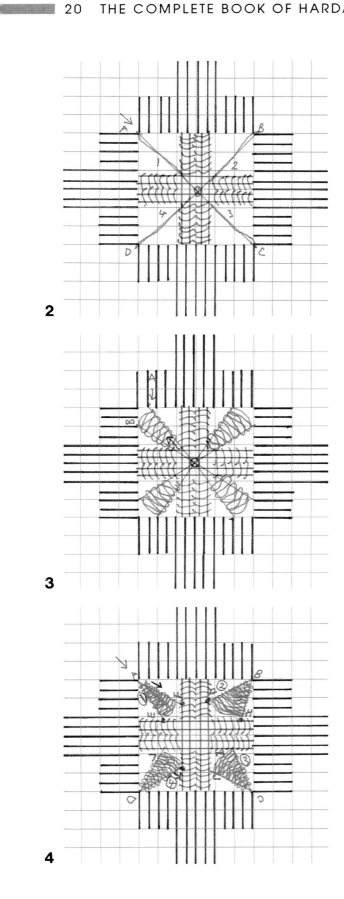

2

2

3

3

4

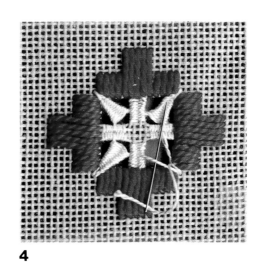

4

Graph 2 and Sample 2

The threads are cut and removed as in Graph A. Needleweave the bars as in Graph 1. To make the spokes, bring the needle up at arrow A, insert it at the centre, up in square 2, down at corner B. Twist this thread twice around spoke just made, as shown in Sample 2. Then insert needle at the centre, bring it up in square 3, insert it at corner C, then twist thread twice. Insert the needle at the centre, up in square 4, down at corner D, twist thread twice, then insert at centre, bring up in square 1, and twist this last thread twice to corner A. Take thread through to finish at back of block.

Graph 3 and Sample 3

The threads are cut and removed as in Graph A. After needleweaving the bars, bring the needle up at arrow A, then insert at centre O, and take up at B. Twist this thread once, then insert the needle at centre O and bring up between the two threads that have just been made. Needleweave these two threads from centre to A and B, as shown in Sample 3, then take the thread down and carry to the wrong side and come up in the centre block of the next square. Repeat until all four squares are completed.

Graph 4 and Sample 4

The threads are cut and removed as in Graph A. First square: Bring needle up at A (see arrow), then insert in the middle of the bar at E, twist the thread once. Insert the needle into the fabric at A and up in square 1, insert into the middle of bar F, twist back to A, insert into the fabric at A, and come up in between the two spokes. Needleweave over and under these two until completed, finishing at F. Take the thread from F to G to make the second square.

Second square: Bring the needle from G to corner B, then insert it into the fabric and up into square 2. Take thread to middle of bar H, twist back to B, insert needle into fabric and up in between spokes. Needleweave, finishing at H. Then take the needle to I and insert at corner C and bring up in square 3. Complete third and fourth square as above, finishing with the thread at back of the block.

Graph 5 and Sample 5

The threads are cut and removed as in Graph A. Needleweave to half-way along bar 1. Make a picot, as illustrated in Sample 5, on both sides. Complete bar with needleweaving. Insert the needle diagonally to the second bar and need-

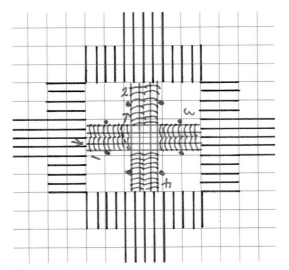

5

5

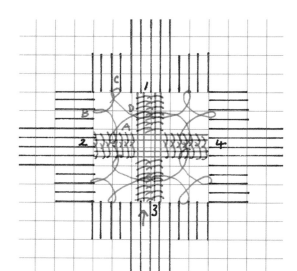

6

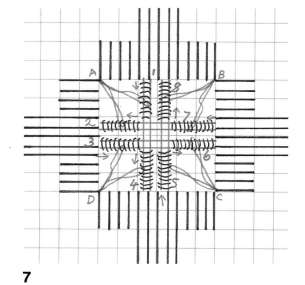

7

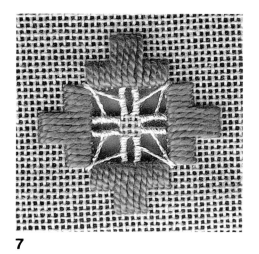

6

7

leweave to half-way along this bar. Make a picot on both sides. Complete needleweaving. Insert the needle and run the thread at the back of the block to the third bar. Complete all four bars.

Graph 6 and Sample 6

Dove's Eye

The threads are cut and removed as in Graph A. Needleweave bar 1 completely and bar 2 to half-way. Take the thread over and under between A to D; D to C; C to B and B to A. Finish needleweaving bar 2. The threads should cross on all four sides the same way. When working clockwise, the right thread is on top. See Sample 6. When taking the thread into the blocks, stab into the centre of the satin stitch rather than in between the satin stitches, so that they will not be separated. To start second Dove's Eye, take the thread from bar 2 around the back of the block to bar 3, then needleweave to half-way along this bar and work the Dove's Eye as described above, working clockwise. Finish needleweaving bar 3, and move diagonally to bar 4. Needleweave to half-way along this bar and work the third Dove's Eye. Work the fourth Dove's Eye before finishing the needleweaving on bar 4. Finish off thread at back of block.

Graph 7 and Sample 7

The threads are cut and removed as in Graph A. All the bars in this block are corded (wrapped) over two threads, as shown by the arrows and numbers on the graph. Cord bar 1 to half-way then take the thread to corner A. Twist back to bar 1 (see graph for method of twisting) and finish cording this bar. Take the thread diagonally to bar 2 and cord it to half-way. Take the thread to corner A, then twist back to bar 2 and complete the cording. Take thread to bar 3, cord

it to half-way, then take thread to corner D. Twist back to bar 3 and finish cording this bar. Take thread diagonally to bar 4 and cord this one to half-way then take the thread back to corner D. Twist back to bar 4 and finish cording this bar. Take thread from bar 4 to bar 5 and follow instructions for corners C and B.

Graph 8 and Sample 8

Threads are cut and removed as shown in Graph B. Commence with the eyelet at the arrow marked on the graph. Insert the needle at the centre and bring it up in the next thread, continuing around to the beginning. Then cord the top two threads to the next eyelet. Work all four sides, then cord 3 1/2 bars of the inner threads, before working a Dove's Eye, as described in Graph 6. Finish cording the last bar.

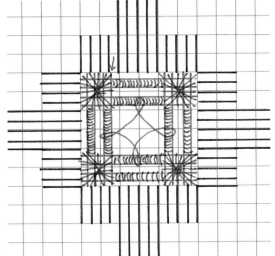

8

8

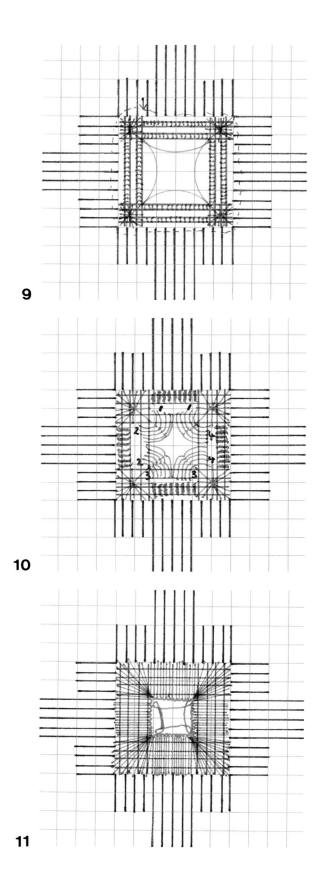

9

10

11

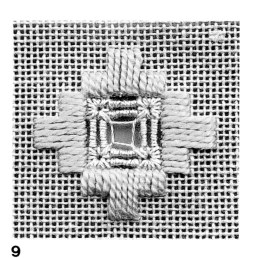

9

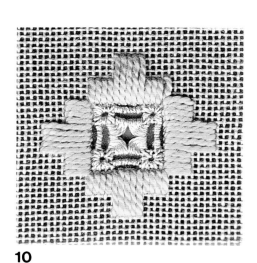

10

11

Graph 9 and Sample 9

Threads are cut and removed as shown in Graph B. Commence with the eyelet and cording as described in Graph 8. Cord the inner two threads on all four sides. Bring the needle up in the corner of the last corded bar then insert it into the next corner, bring the needle out between the bar and the thread and go to next corner. Finish the four sides and take the thread through to the back to finish off.

Graph 10 and Sample 10

Threads are cut and removed as shown in Graph B. Follow instructions for Graph 8 for the outside row.

Take the needle to the corner and needleweave over and under bar 1 and bar 2 to half-way. Then take the needle over to the next corner and needleweave bars 2 and 3, thus completing bar 2, but working bar 3 to half-way only (see graph).

Take the needle to the corner and needleweave over and under bars 3 and 4 to half-way only. Then take the needle to the next corner, needleweave bars 1 and 4 and finish at back of work.

Graph 11 and Sample 11

Threads are cut and removed as in Graph B. Buttonhole **inwards** (see graph) all around the corners in every thread and bar. Make a square Dove's Eye as shown in Graph 9.

Graph 12 and Sample 12

Cut and remove threads as shown in Graph A. Needleweave bar 1 completely and bar 2 to half-way. Insert the needle into centre of bar 1, up into the centre of bar 2 then back again into bar 1. Buttonhole over the three threads just made and count the stitches, as all four sides have to be the same size.

Finish needleweaving bar 2. Carry thread through the back to bar 3. Needleweave this bar to half-way then take the thread from bar 3 to bar 2, back to bar 3, then back to bar 2. Buttonhole over these three threads, then needleweave the remainder of bar 3. Take the thread through the back to bar 4. Needleweave to half-way then take threads as described above. Buttonhole back to bar 4 then take three threads to bar 1 and buttonhole back to bar 4 and finish needleweaving this bar.

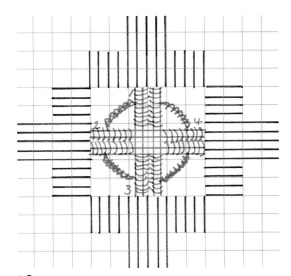

12

12

Graph 13 and Sample 13

Cut and remove threads as in Graph A. All bars are corded over two threads. Cord bar 1 to half-way, then take the thread to corner A (see sample), then twist back to bar 1. Needleweave from the corner over and under bar 1 and bar 2 to half-way. Take the thread to corner A, then twist back to bar 2 and finish cording bar 2. Take the thread to bar 3 and follow instructions as above for all squares. See arrows on graph for direction of cording bars.

Graph 14 and Sample 14

Cut and remove threads as in Graph B. Button-hole around corners and along bars towards the blocks on all four sides. Bring the needle to a centre of one of the bars and make a Dove's Eye.

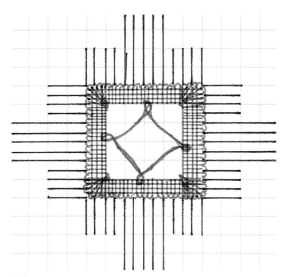

14

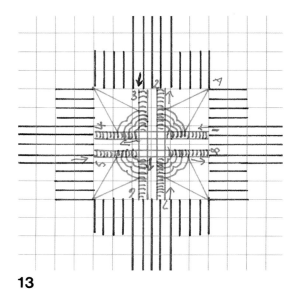

13

14

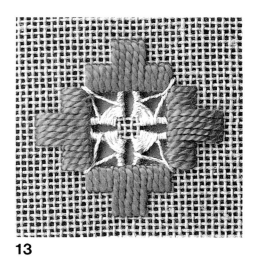

13

Graph 15 and Sample 15

Cut and remove threads as in Graph B. The outer two threads are corded and joined by eyelets in each corner. The inner two threads are needlewoven on all four sides. Then take the thread from corner to corner and needleweave over two opposite threads.

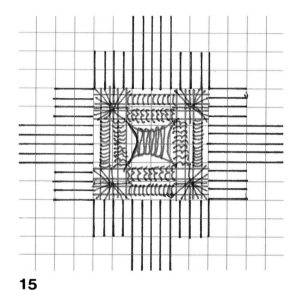

15

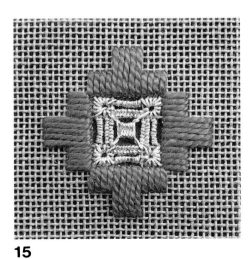

15

Graph 16 and Sample 16

Cut and remove threads as in Graph B. Make an eyelet in each corner, then needleweave the bars and add picots as described in Graph 5.

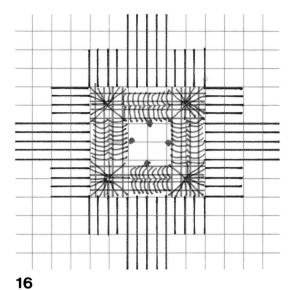

16

16

Graph 17 and Sample 17

Cut and remove threads as in Graph B.
Commence first eyelet at arrow. Needleweave
over and under one thread of each bar.

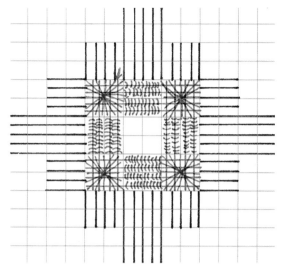

17

17

Graph 18 and Sample 18

Spider's Web

Cut and remove threads as in Graph A. Cord
over two threads around the block, as shown in
Graph 7. Make spokes as shown in Graph 2,
except that in the last spoke the needle stays in
the centre to begin the web. There are four
spokes and 8 corded bars. Weave over two bars
and under one spoke in a clockwise direction
until the web is formed. Finish at the untwisted
bar, then twist it and finish at back of work.

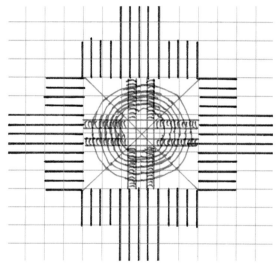

18

18

Graph 19 and Sample 19

Follow instructions for Graph 18, but weave over one spoke and under two bars in an anti-clockwise direction until the web shows on the back. Finish off as in graph 18.

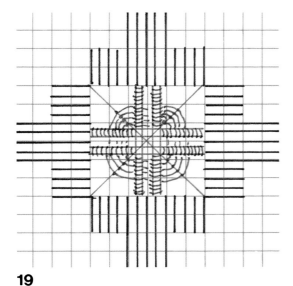

19

19

Graph 20 and Sample 20

Cut and remove threads as in Graph B. Buttonhole around corners and along the outer two threads. Buttonhole inner two threads towards the centre finishing at corner 1. Then take the thread across to corner 2, then twisting at half-way take thread to corner 3. Twist at half-way and tie three spokes with a buttonhole. Take thread to corner 4, twist to centre, make buttonhole and twist back to 1. Finish off at back of block.

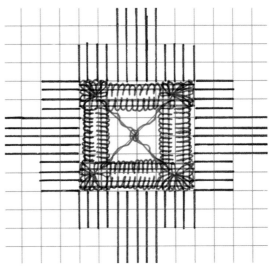

20

20

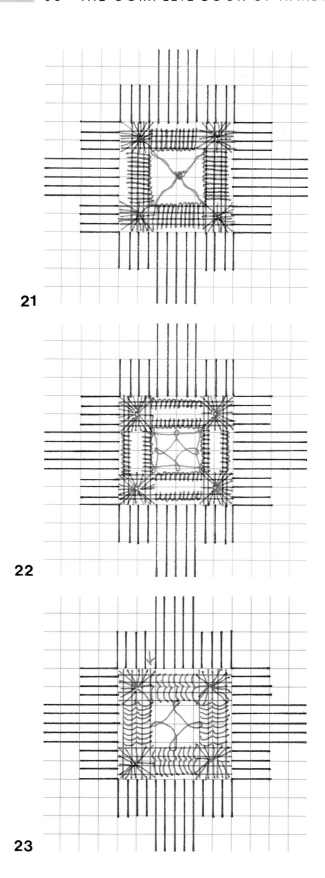

21

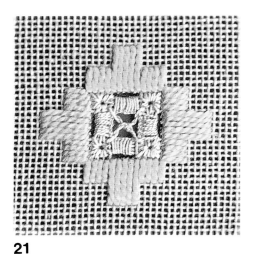

21

22

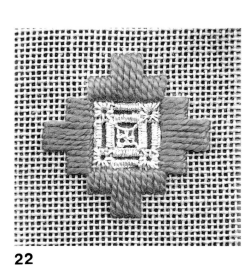

22

23

23

Graph 21 and Sample 21

Cut and remove threads as in Graph B. Make eyelets and buttonhole towards centre over all four threads of the bars. Work centre as shown in Graph 20.

Graph 22 and Sample 22

Cut and remove threads as in Graph B. Make eyelets and buttonhole towards block over two threads on all four sides. Buttonhole inner two threads inwards, then bring needle up in a corner and make loop stitches from corner to corner. Bring needle to the centre of one of the four threads just made and work a Dove's eye.

Graph 23 and Sample 23

Cut and remove threads as in Graph B. Starting at arrow, make eyelets and needleweave 3 1/2 bars. Make Dove's Eye, then complete needleweaving the last bar, finishing with the thread at the back of the work.

Graph 24 and Sample 24

Cut and remove threads as in Graph A. Needleweave the four bars. Take the thread through the back of the block and up at corner A, then insert it at the centre and take back to A. Needleweave between the two threads just made as shown on the graph, following the direction of the arrow. Insert the needle into the fabric at the centre and bring it up at B. Then insert the needle at the centre and bring it up between the two threads just made. Needleweave those threads to B (see arrow). Insert the needle into the fabric at B, take the thread across the back of the work and up at C, then down at the centre and up at C. Needleweave the two threads back to the centre, and take the needle down at D and up at the centre. Needleweave the two threads (see arrow) back to D. Insert the needle into the fabric and finish off at the back of the work.

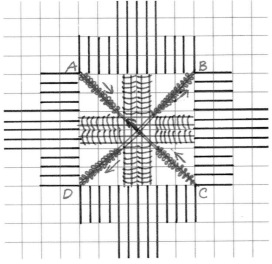

24

24

Graph 25 and Sample 25

Cut and remove threads as in Graph A. Cord over two threads to half-way along bar 1 then make a picot as shown in Sample 5. Finish cording bar 1. Take the thread diagonally to bar 2, then follow the arrows on the graph and Sample 25. Make spokes as illustrated in Graph 2 and Sample 2.

Graph 26 and Sample 26

Cut and remove threads as in Graph A. Follow the instructions given with Graph 6, except that now the bars are needlewoven over two threads instead of over four threads.

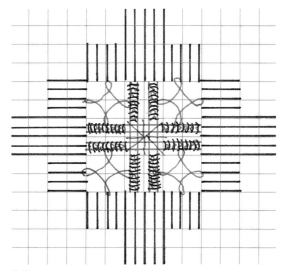

26

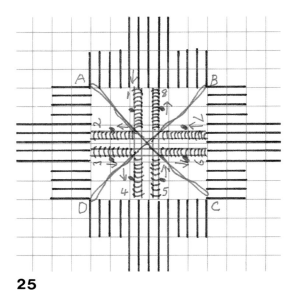

25

26

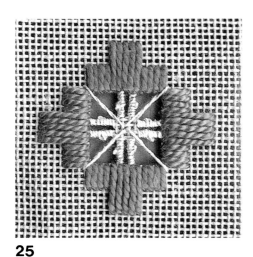

25

Graph 27 and Sample 27

Cut and remove threads as in Graph A. Cord eight bars over two threads. Bring the thread up to the front at A, then to the centre, twist it, then insert the needle at B, bring it up at C, then twist back to A. Take the thread through the back of the block to do the next square and continue until all four are completed.

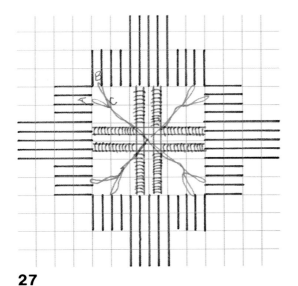

27

27

Graph 28 and Sample 28

Cut and remove threads as in Graph A. Cord over two threads, following arrows on the graph. Bring the thread to corner A and follow instructions given with Graph 2 for diagonal spokes. Bring the needle up at 1 and work anti-clockwise. Pass the needle over diagonal thread to 2 and loop from 2 around to 12 then under 1, as shown on graph. Then pass the needle under and over loops and spokes and bars, all around. Finish thread at back.

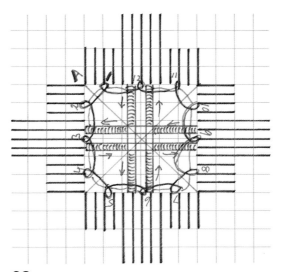

28

28

Graph 29 and Sample 29

Cut and remove threads as in Graph A. Commencing at A, make diagonal spokes following instructions in Graph 2.

Do not twist first spoke. Bring the needle up at the arrow from centre and needleweave over bar 1, the spoke and bar 2, back and forth. Complete all four squares.

Graph 30 and Sample 30

Cut and remove threads as in Graph A. Cord over two threads half-way down bar, then bring needle out between bar A and bar B at centre, and needleweave over and under these two bars. Complete bar B with cording and repeat design on remaining three sides. This design is known as **Maltese Cross**, and Sample 30 shows the embroidery.

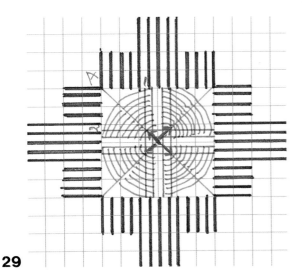

29

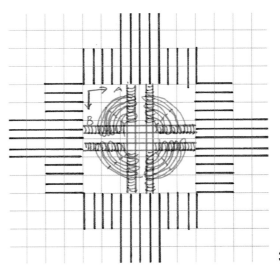

30

29

30

Intermediate

LESSON ONE

Reverse Faggot

Graphs 1A, 1B, 1C and Samples 1A, 1B, 1C
and 1D.

This stitch is worked diagonally over 2 FT,
and consists of two rows. Following Graphs 1A
and 1B, bring needle up at A, insert at B, come
up at C, down at D, up at B, down at E.
Continue to desired length. See Sample 1A for
movement of the needle. See Samples 1C
and 1D for turning the corner.

1A

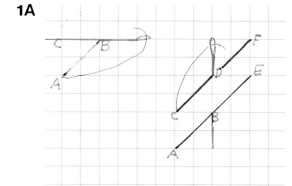

1B

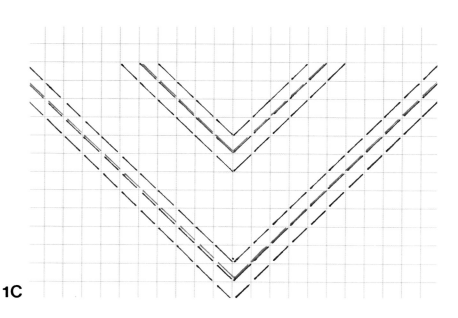

1C

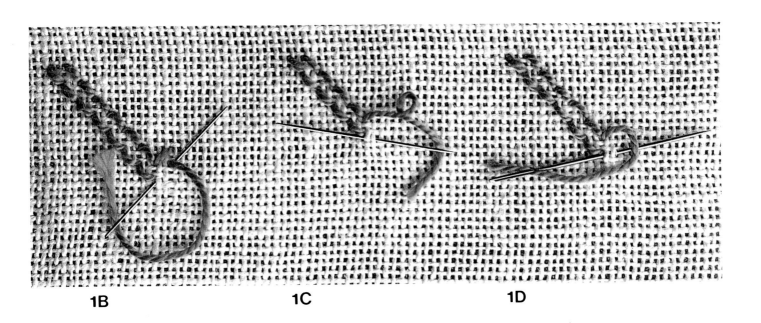

1B **1C** **1D**

LESSON TWO

The following designs are enclosed within Kloster blocks of varying shapes. Each graph details the method of working the Kloster blocks.

Sampler Two

This sampler shows ten different blocks and needleweaving. The borders are buttonholed in four different ways.

Graph 1

Kloster blocks for graphs 1 to 4 are worked as follows:
4 SS over 4 FT
5 SS over 8 FT
4 SS over 4 FT made into a square.
Graph 1 shows FT cut and removed as in Graph B. Needleweave two bars with cross stitch in corners. Cord two bars with cross stitch in corners. Needleweave the inside two threads as shown in sample.

Graph 2

Cut and remove two threads at corners and four in the centre. Needleweave remaining two threads from 1 to 2 and 3 to 4, as shown in graph and sample. Complete all four squares.

Graph 3

Cut and remove threads as in Graph A. Cord over two threads for the eight bars, as shown, then make the Dove's Eyes as described in Chapter 2, Graph 6.

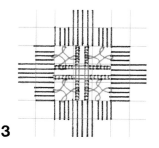

1

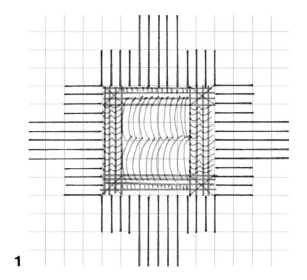

2

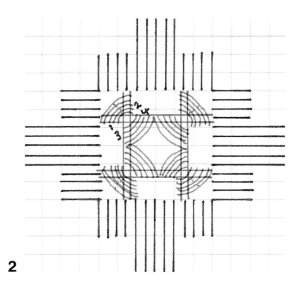

3

Graph 4

Cut and remove threads as in Graph A. Needleweave over two threads over eight bars, and make Dove's Eyes as described in Chapter 2, Graph 6.

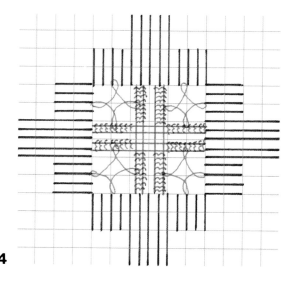

4

Graph 5

Make block as follows:

1 SS over 10 FT	1 SS over 5 FT
1 SS over 9 FT	1 SS over 6 FT
1 SS over 8 FT	1 SS over 7 FT
1 SS over 7 FT	1 SS over 8 FT
1 SS over 6 FT	1 SS over 9 FT
1 SS over 5 FT	1 SS over 10 FT
5 SS over 4 FT	

All four sides are worked as above, forming a square. Remove all threads in this square. Make spokes as follows: Bring needle up at A, insert at B, up into square, down at D, twist back to B, up into square and down at C, twist back to B, come up into square and take down at E. Twist back to B, up into square and down to F, then twist back to B. Bring needle out on the side of the spokes and needleweave over and under the five spokes to half-way, then under and over the three centre spokes, finishing in centre spoke. Twist thread and finish at back of work.

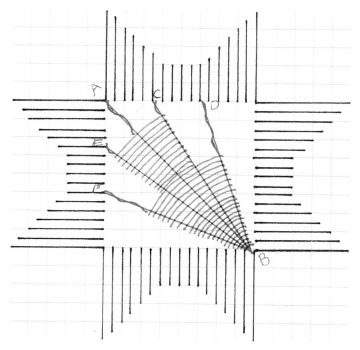

5

Graph 6

Make block as follows:

4 SS over 4 FT

4 SS over 8 FT

5 SS over 8 FT, but 4 FT higher than previous 4 SS over 8 FT

Drop down 4 FT again and make 4 SS over 8 FT

4 SS over 4 FT.

Make four sides as above to form a square. Make eyelets in open space between the two groups of 4 SS over 8 FT. See graph.

Cut and remove eight threads on all corners*.

Cord over two threads and make Dove's Eyes as described in Chapter 2, Graph 6.

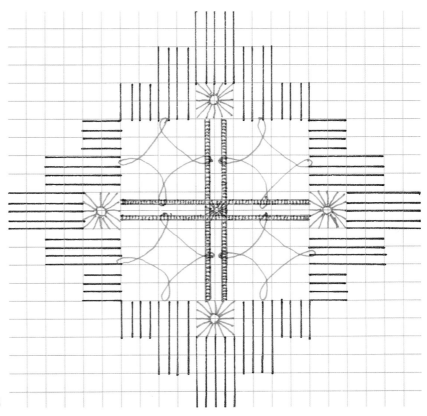

6

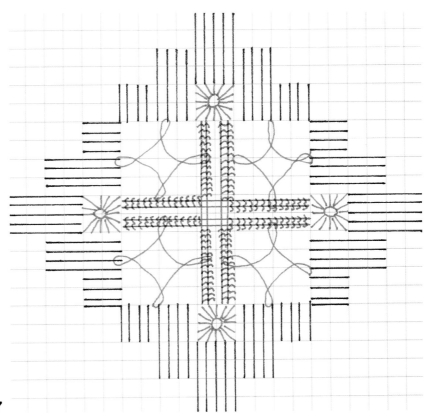

Graph 7

Follow instructions for Graph 6 to *, then needleweave over two threads and make Dove's Eyes as described in Chapter 2, Graph 6.

7

Graph 8

Make block as follows:

5 SS over 4 FT	1 SS over 7 FT
1 SS over 5 FT	1 SS over 6 FT
1 SS over 6 FT	1 SS over 5 FT
1 SS over 7 FT	5 SS over 4 FT
1 SS over 8 FT	
1 SS over 9 FT	
1 SS over 10 FT	
1 SS over 9 FT	
1 SS over 8 FT	

Work four sides as above to form a square. Cut and remove eight threads on all corners. Cord over the remaining four threads. Bring the needle up at the arrow, insert at centre, then up in square 1 at position 1. Insert needle at centre and twist back. Bring needle to position 2, then insert at centre and bring needle from centre to square and needleweave to top, ending at centre spoke. Twist this thread, then take needle through back of the block to come up at corner B. Repeat as above to finish all four squares.

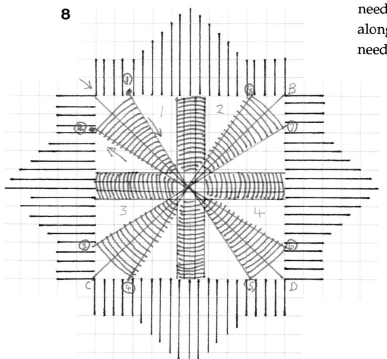

Graph 9

Make block as follows:

4 SS over 4 FT	4 SS over 8 FT
4 SS over 8 FT	4 SS over 4 FT
5 SS over 12 FT	

Make four sides as above to form a square. Cut and remove eight threads on all corners and needleweave bars 1 and 2 over two threads. Bring needle up at corner of bar 2 and make loop stitches as shown on graph and sample. Then run thread over and under these loop stitches. Complete all four squares.

Graph 10

Make a square block as in Graph 9. Cut 4 FT, leave 4 FT, cut 4 FT, leave 4 FT, cut 4 FT. There are now two bars of 4 FT on each side of the block.
Cord over two threads of bar 1 to half-way only. Bring needle to corner and needleweave over and under bars 1 and 2, the latter only to half-way, then finish bar 2 with cording. Bring needle to bar 3, cord to half-way, take needle to corner and needleweave half-way along bar 3 and half-way along bar 4. Take needle to corner of bars 4 and 5. Needleweave over bars 4 and 5. See graph. Continue instructions around the blocks, following arrows for directions.
Make four eyelets as shown in the graph and sample. Cord three centre bars completely, then the remaining one to half-way. Make Dove's Eye then complete the cording on the last bar.

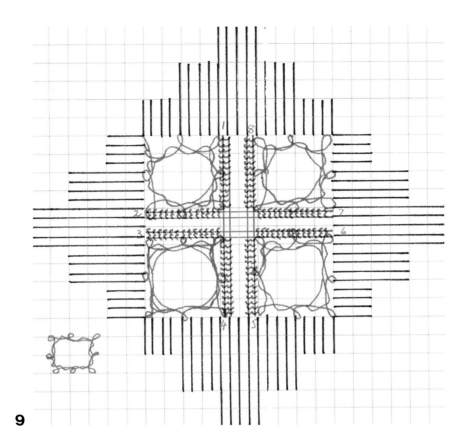

9

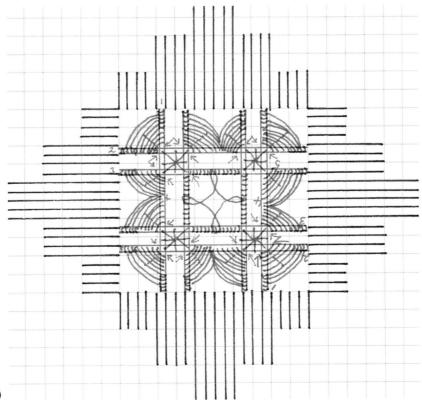

10

LESSON THREE

Sampler Three

This sampler shows various ways of needleweaving borders that are suitable for framing designs. They are self explanatory. For instructions, see separate sampler.

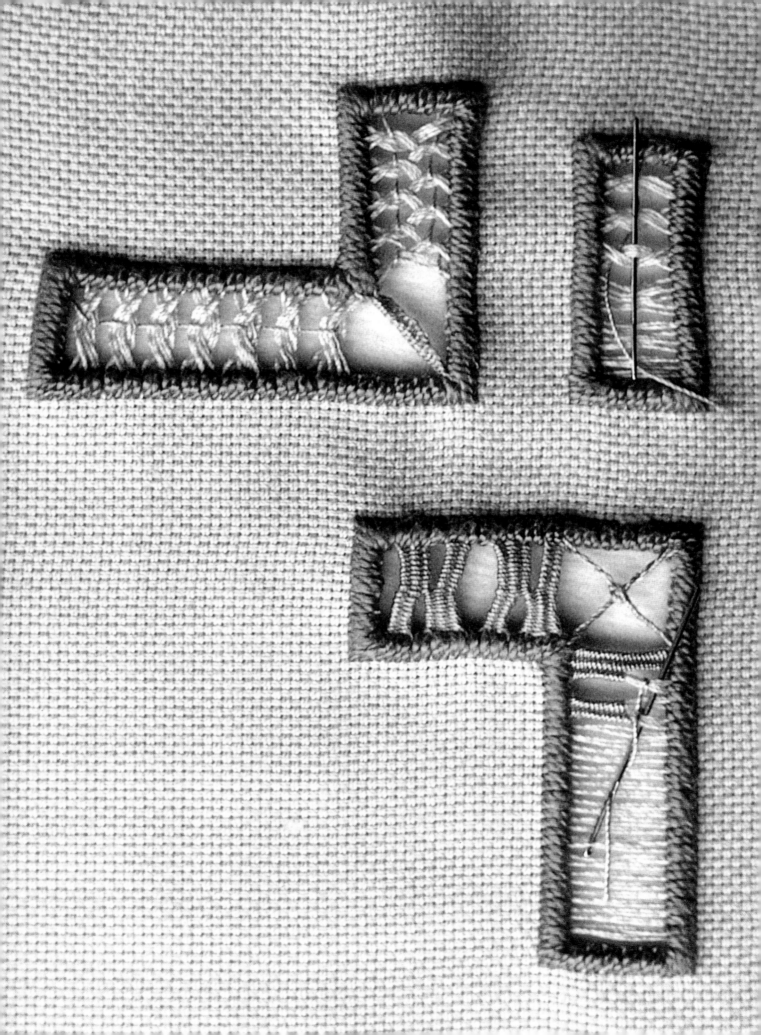

LESSON FOUR

Sampler Four

EYELETS Various effects can be obtained by using different methods, shapes and sizes as shown in the separate sampler marked C.

LESSON FIVE | Sampler Five

DECORATIVE MOTIFS   See graphs 1 to 20 for stars, squares and various shapes.

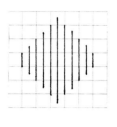

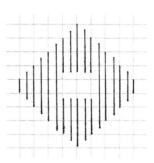

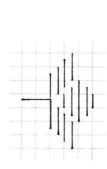

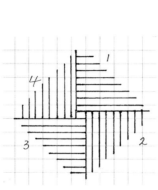

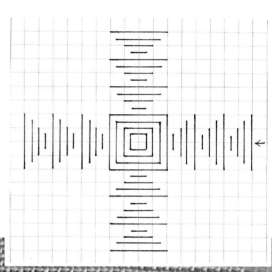

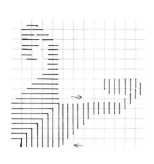

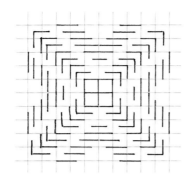

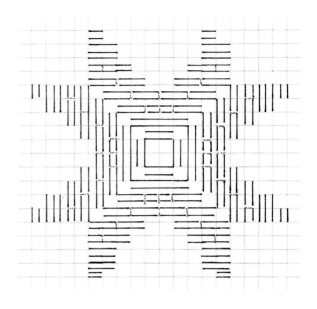

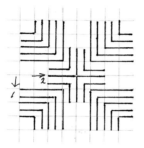

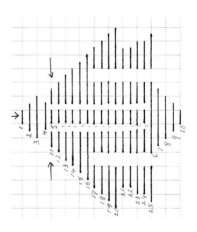

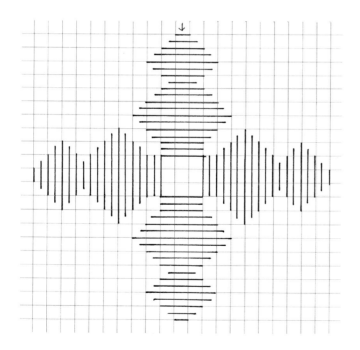

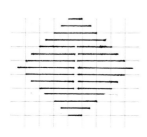

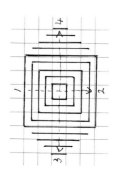

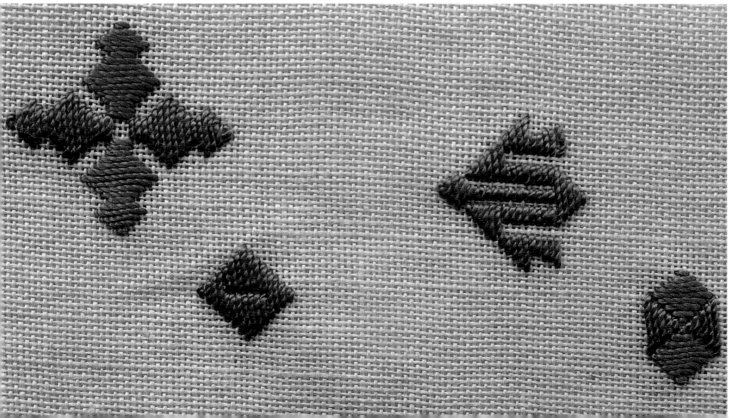

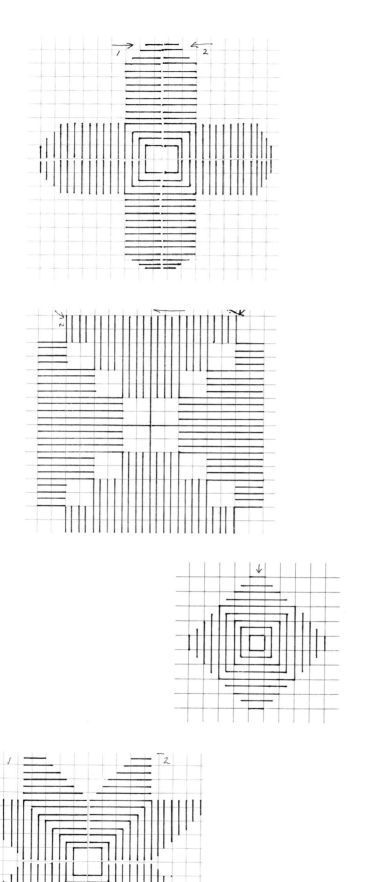
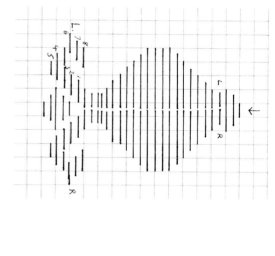
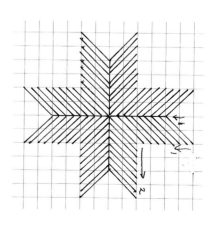

CHAPTER FOUR

Advanced Designs and Graphs

Sampler Six

Graph 1

Begin at arrow and make 5 vertical stitches as follows:

1 SS over 4 FT
1 SS over 5 FT
1 SS over 6 FT

1 SS over 5 FT
1 SS over 4 FT

Make a square so that the horizontal and vertical stitches meet in the same hole (see sample). Miss four threads and make 5 SS over 4 FT. Make second block, then repeat on other three sides.

Cut four threads, as indicated by the blue line on graph, then cut threads in corresponding open squares on graph. Remaining bars are buttonholed inwards. Make a loop stitch in four squares. Centre square has spokes and wheel.

Graph 2

Work square as follows:

5 SS over 4 FT
Miss 4 FT
2 SS over 4 FT
2 SS over 6 FT
5 SS over 8 FT

2 SS over 6 FT
2 SS over 4 FT
Miss 4 FT
5 SS over 4 FT

Make sure that the horizontal and vertical stitches on corners meet in the same hole. Cut four threads, leaving three times four threads. Bars 1, 2, 3 and 4 are buttonholed and become twisted. All others are needlewoven, except the four centre bars.

The centre spider's web is described in graphs 2 and 18 in Chapter 2, and is woven over these four bars and spokes. Samples 3, 4, 5, 6 and 7 show how picots, eyelets, Dove's eyes and needlewoven corners are used in differently shaped blocks.

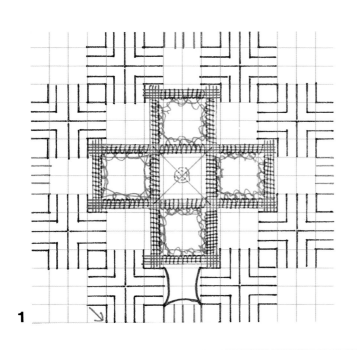

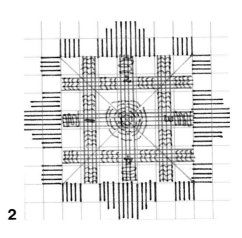

LESSON TWO

Sampler Seven

Graph 1 and Sample 1

Commence with square of Kloster blocks
as follows:

1 SS over 4 FT
1 SS over 5 FT
1 SS over 6 FT
1 SS over 5 FT
1 SS over 4 FT

Continue making these five stitches in
diagonal fashion, making sure the third, fifth
and seventh block meet with previous block
stitches, as shown on the graph and sample.
Cut FT as indicated. Bars are all needlewoven
with picots in the middle of the outsides.
Instructions for Dove's Eyes are given in
Chapter 2, Graph 6.

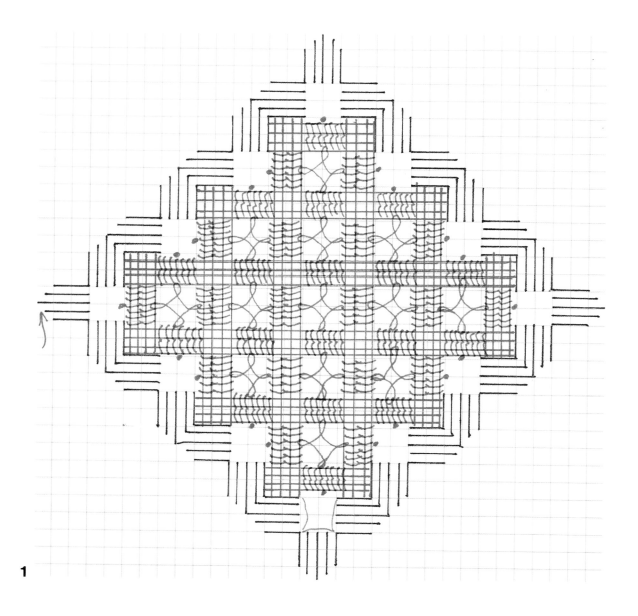

1

Graph 2 and Samples 2 and 2a

Commence with a square of Kloster
blocks as follows:

	1 SS over 6 FT
1 SS over 4 FT	1 SS over 7 FT
1 SS over 5 FT	1 SS over 8 FT
1 SS over 6 FT	1 SS over 7 FT
1 SS over 7 FT	1 SS over 6 FT
1 SS over 8 FT	1 SS over 5 FT
1 SS over 7 FT	1 SS over 4 FT,

leave 4 FT and repeat twice. Make all four
sides the same to form a square. Follow
sampler in yellow and green embroidery.

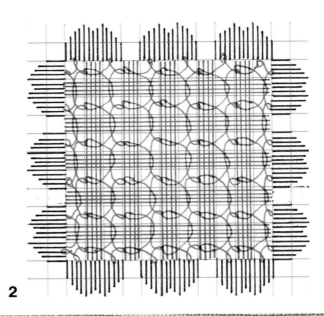

2

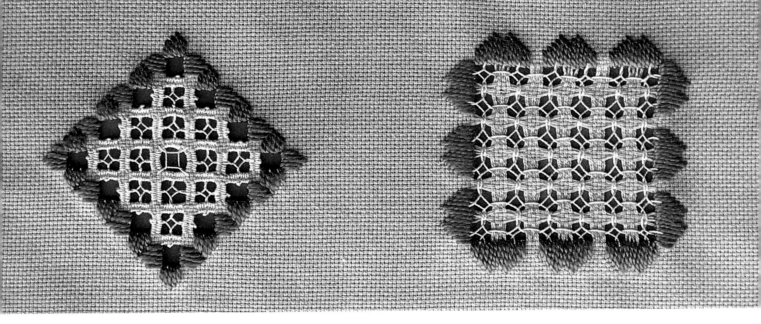

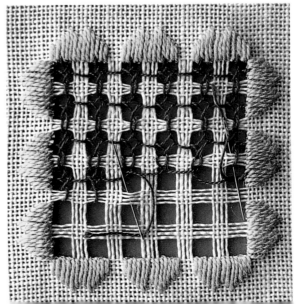

2A

LESSON THREE

Sampler Eight

Graph 1 and Sample 1

Commence with outline of Kloster block:

4 SS over 4 FT
4 SS over 6 FT
4 SS over 8 FT
5 SS over 10 FT

4 SS over 8 FT
4 SS over 6 FT
4 SS over 4 FT.

Cut 6 FT
Leave 4 FT
Cut 8 FT
Leave 4 FT
Cut 6 FT.

Bars 1 to 8 are corded over four threads. Take thread around back to corner A, insert at B, then twist back to A. Bring needle around back and come up at C, insert at D, then twist to 1, and buttonhole towards outside on all four sides. Take the needle to the centre and needleweave over two centre threads. Complete twisting to C. Work loopstitches as in Chapter Two, Lesson Two, Graph 28.

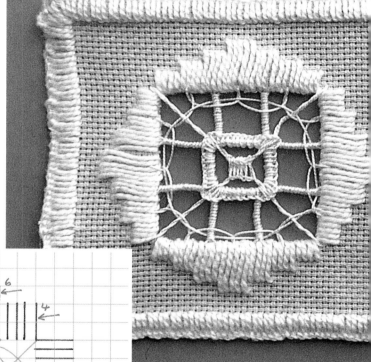

1

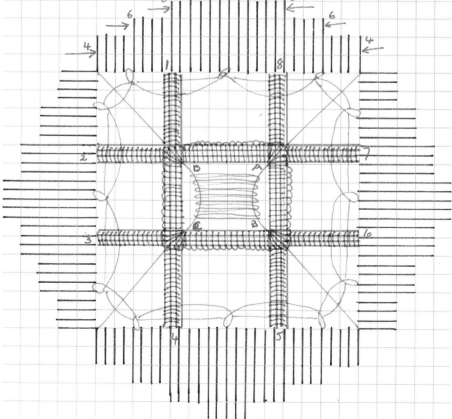

1

Graph 2 and Sample 2

Commence with outline of Kloster block as shown in Graph 1.

Cut and remove four times 4 FT, leaving 4 FT in between (see graph). Cord bars 1 and 2 over four threads. Bring needle across back of block to bar 3 and cord over two threads only. Cord bar 4 over four threads. Take thread to corner at arrow and needleweave over and under bars 4, 2 and 1. Make all four corners as above. Cord bar 5 over four threads and bar 6 over two threads. Cord bar 7 over two threads to halfway and work a Dove's Eye as in Chapter 2, graph 6. Repeat for three other inside squares.

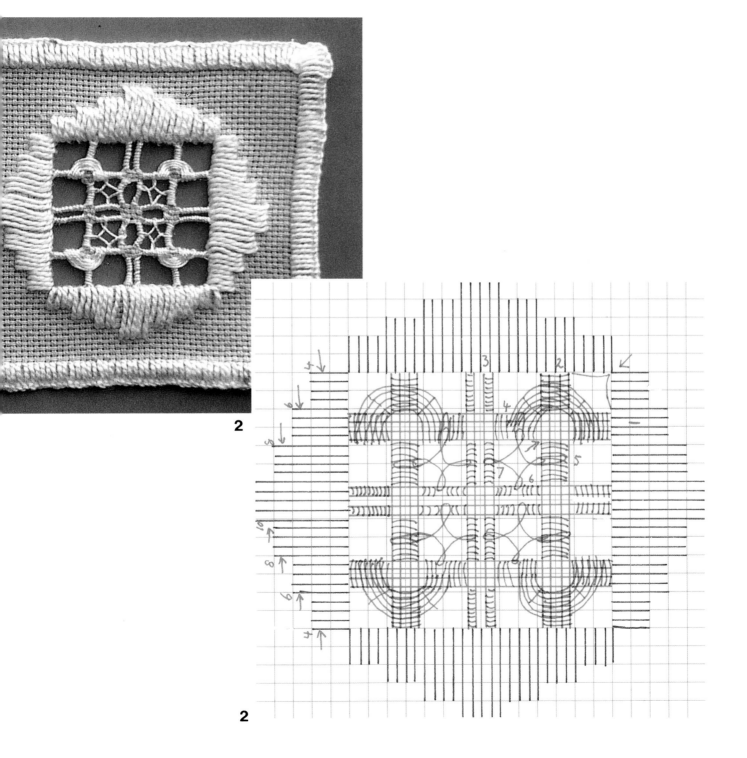

2

2

LESSON FOUR

Sampler Nine

Graph 1 and Sample

Commence with outline of Kloster block:
Make 1 SS each over 3, 4, 5, 6, 5, 4 and 3 FT until
there are forty-nine stitches on each side.

Cut 4 FT, leave 4 FT
Cut 8 FT, leave 4 FT
Cut 8 FT, leave 4 FT
Cut 8 FT, leave 4 FT
Cut 4 FT

Needleweave bar 1 and needleweave to half-
way along bar 2. Make Dove's Eye as shown in
Chapter 2, Graph 6. Complete bar 2. Take
needle back to bar 3 and needleweave over four
threads. Needleweave bar 4 over two threads,
and bar 5 over four threads. Take needle across
back of work to bar 6 and needleweave over
four threads, then needleweave bar 7 to half-
way over four threads, work a Dove's Eye, then
complete bar. Work all four sides.

To work centre: needleweave bars A and B over
two threads. Bring needle to the corner of A and
B and make a spoke from corner to arrow. Twist
back to the corner and needleweave over the
spoke and along bars A and B and two threads
of bar C. Cord over D, E and to half-way along
bar F, make Dove's Eye, then complete bar F.
Repeat in all squares except the centre. Needleweave from corner to corner over the two
remaining threads shown in the centre square
on the graph.

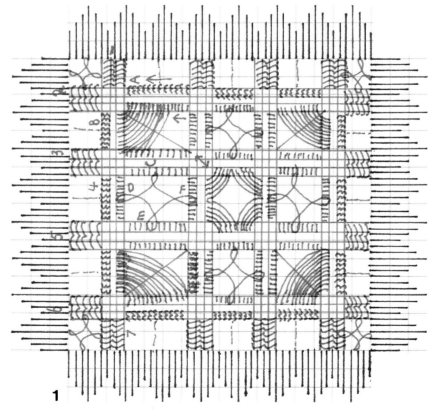

1

1

Graph 2 and Sample 2

Commence with outline of Kloster block:

5 SS over 4 FT, leave 4 FT

2 SS over 4 FT

2 SS over 6 FT

5 SS over 8 FT

2 SS over 6 FT

2 SS over 4 FT

Repeat once more in reverse, leaving
4 FT in between (see graph). Cut 4 FT
and leave 4 FT, alternately.

Work eight Maltese Crosses, as described in
Chapter 2, Graph 30, with two bars of cording
over two threads in between each cross.
Work eyelets in each intersection, when
moving from one bar to the next.
Inner Square: Needleweave over all bars.
Then work needlewoven diagonal bars, as
described in Chapter 2, Lesson 2, Graph 24.

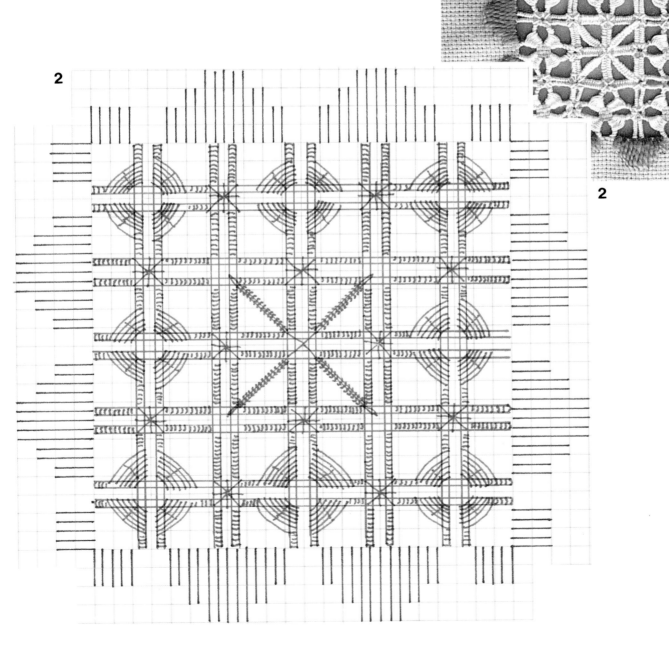

2

CHAPTER FIVE

Twenty-five Projects

The author presents a gallery of her designs made into beautiful and useful pieces, together with graphs where appropriate.

Project A

Whilst this shows simplicity in design, it demonstrates a pleasant use of colours.

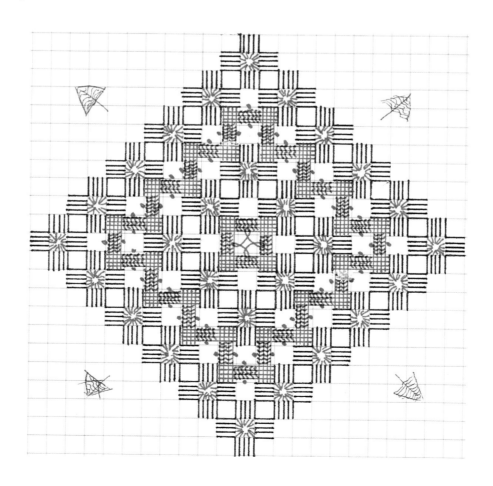

Project B

This demonstrates three different methods of needleweaving with a central motif in each square.

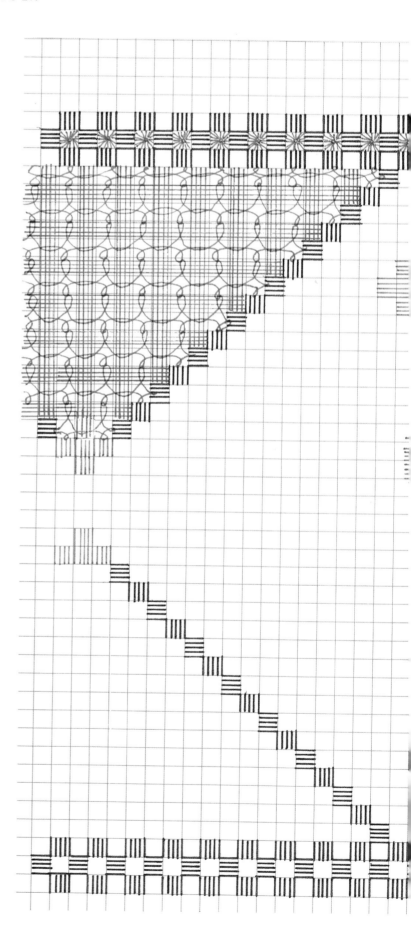

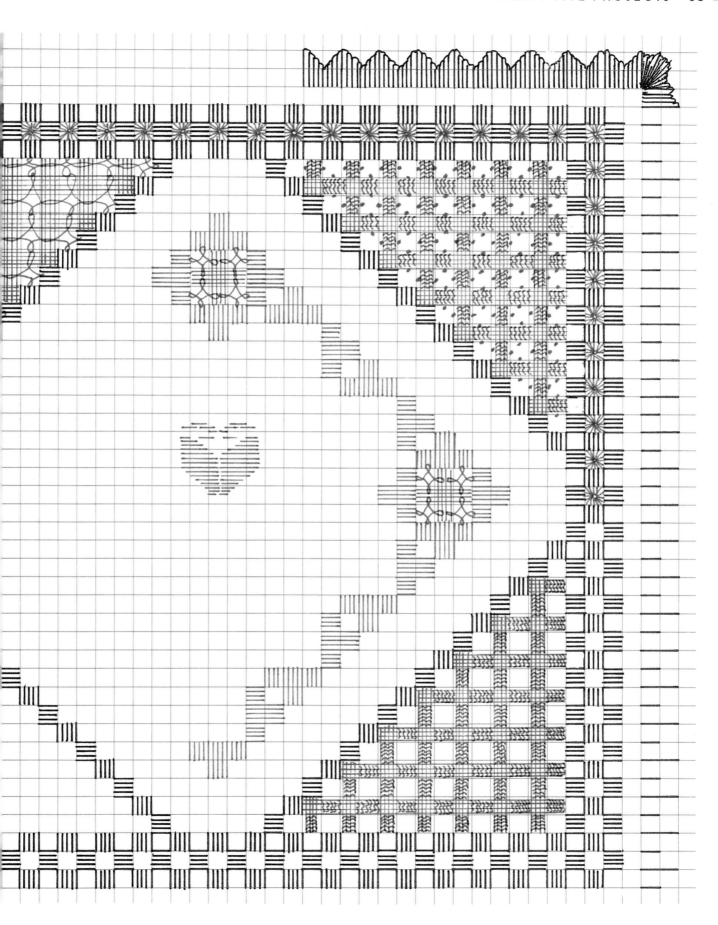

Project C

Small brown table-centre showing various
ways of needleweaving and centre faggoting.

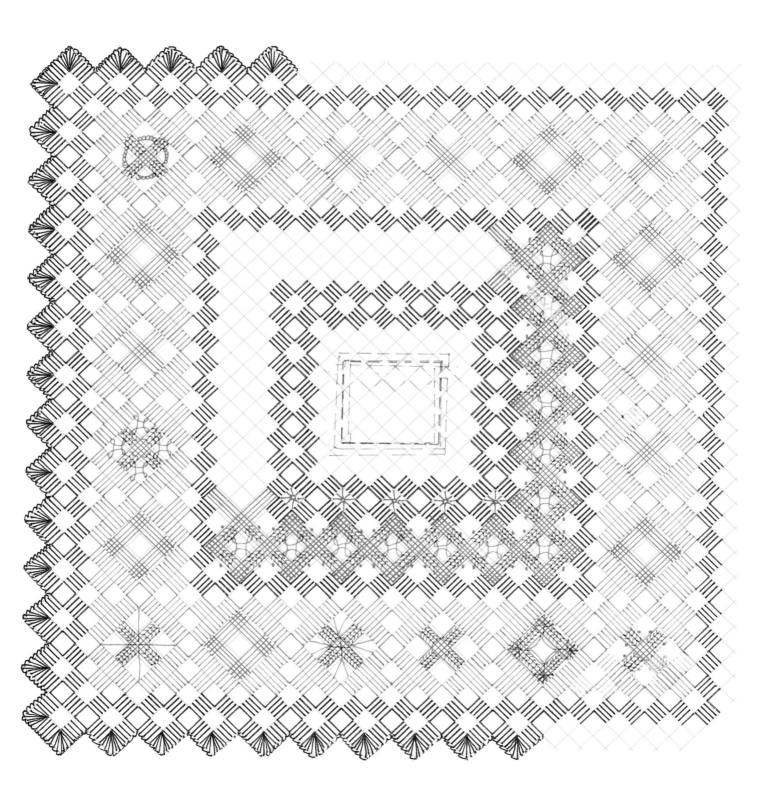

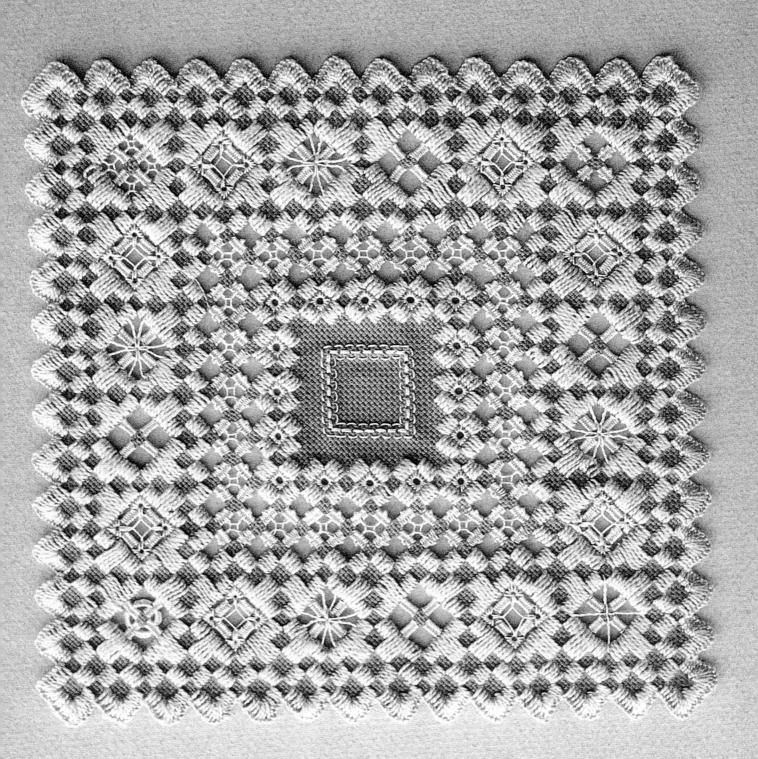

Project D

Octagonal mat in shades of pink and white.

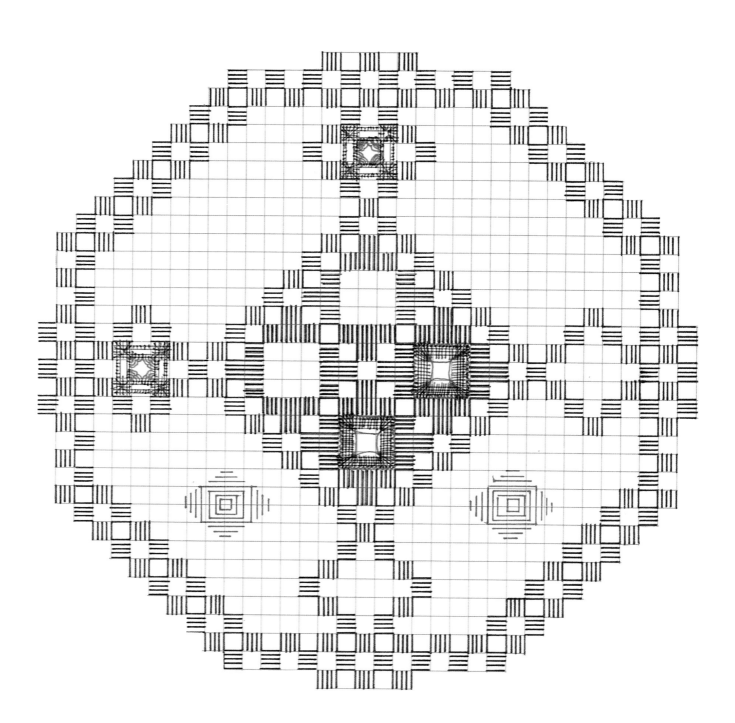

Project E

An off-white bookmark showing
inverted Maltese Cross and Dove's Eyes.

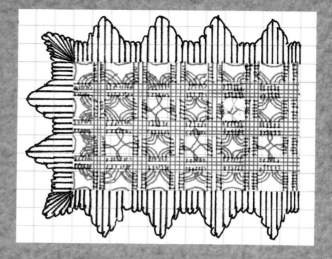

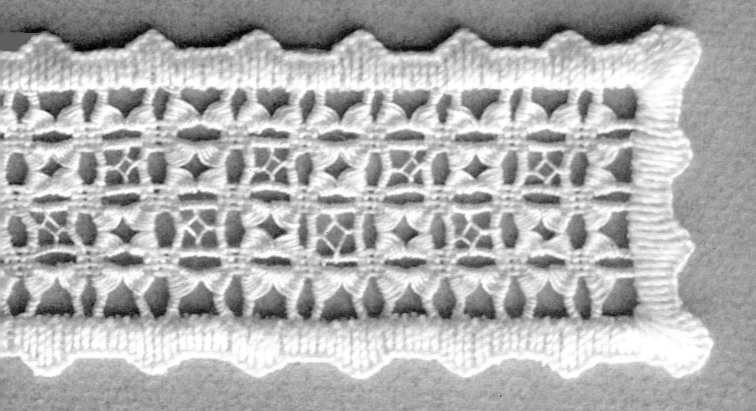

Project F

Shows details of eight
different ways of needle
weaving in an 8-pointed star.

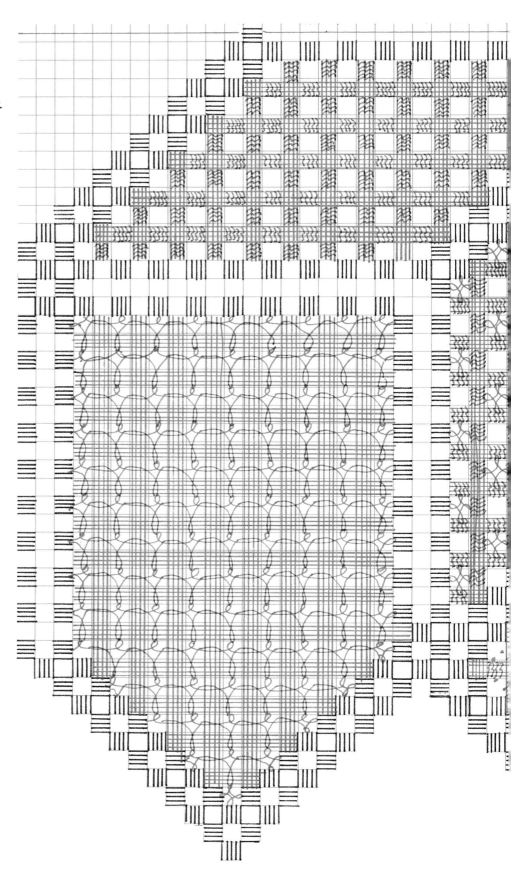

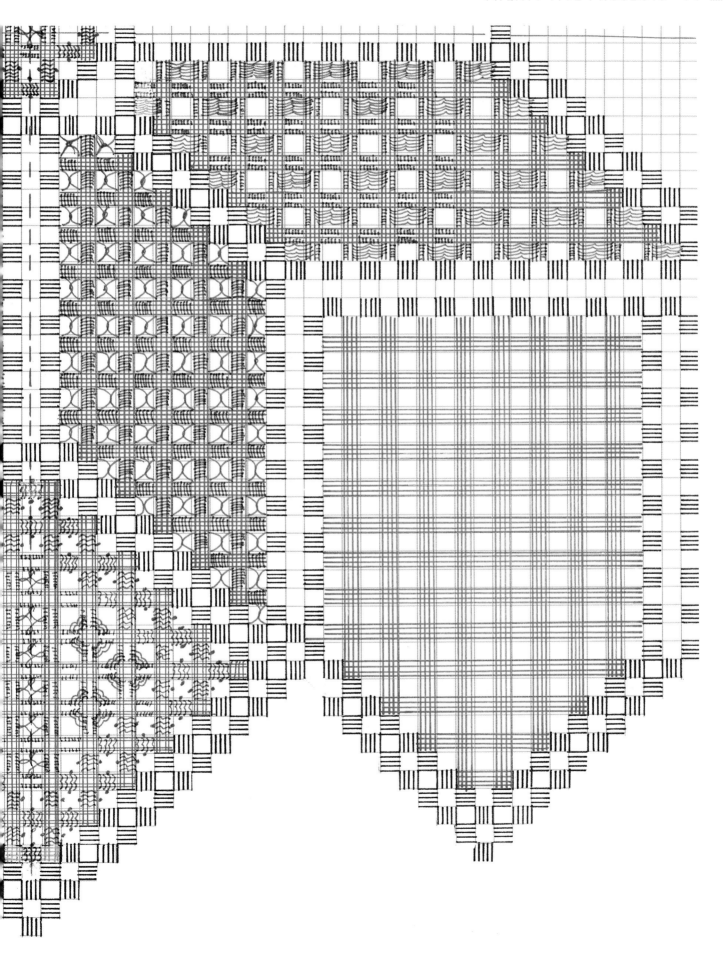

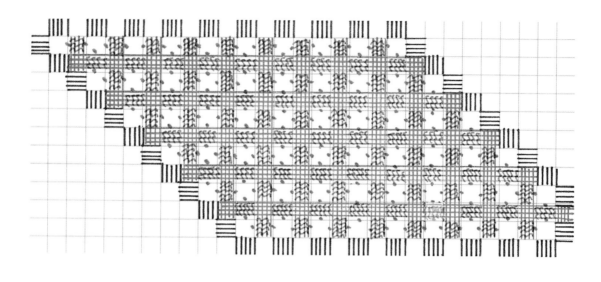

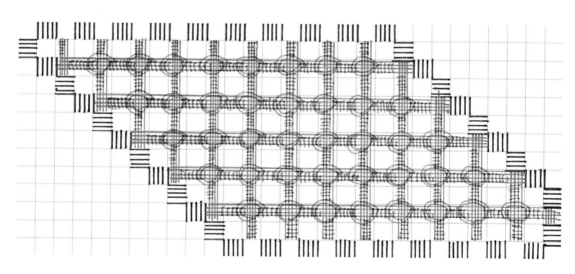

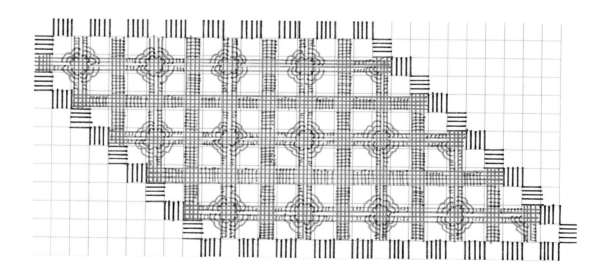

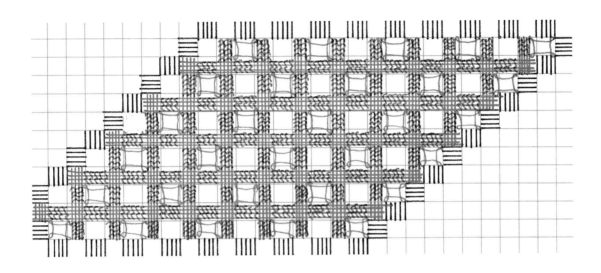

Project G

Table-centre in salmon pink,
show lacy edging, Maltese
Crosses and double row of
fagotting in centre square.

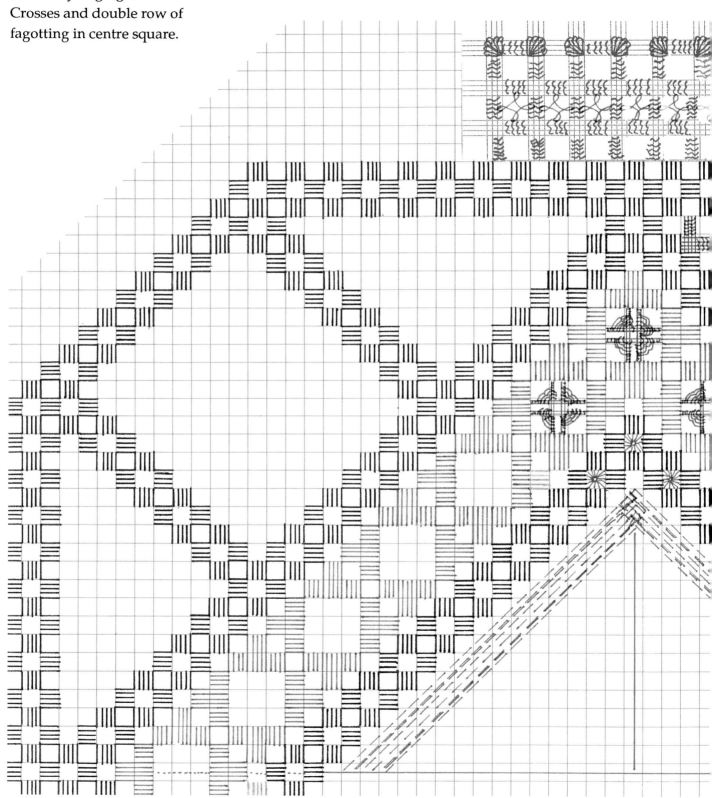

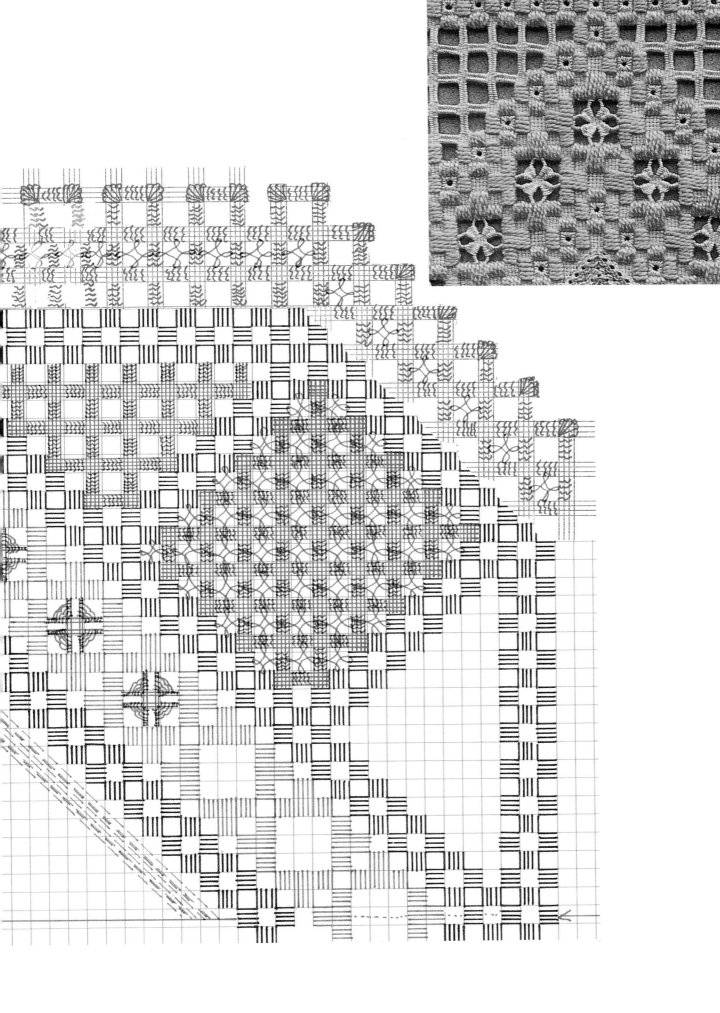

Project H

Demonstrates use of all thirty samples
found in Chapter 2, Lesson 2.

Project I

Follows graphs 1 to 8.

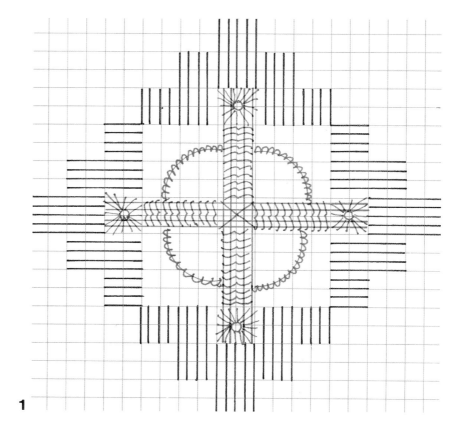

1

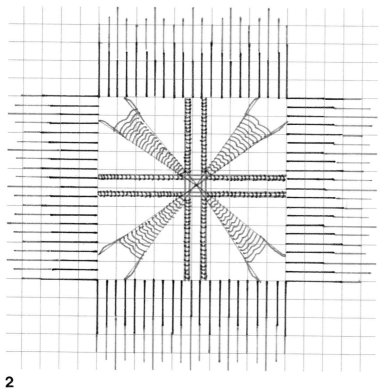

2

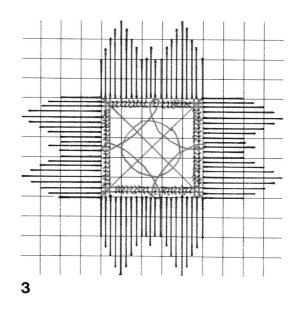

3

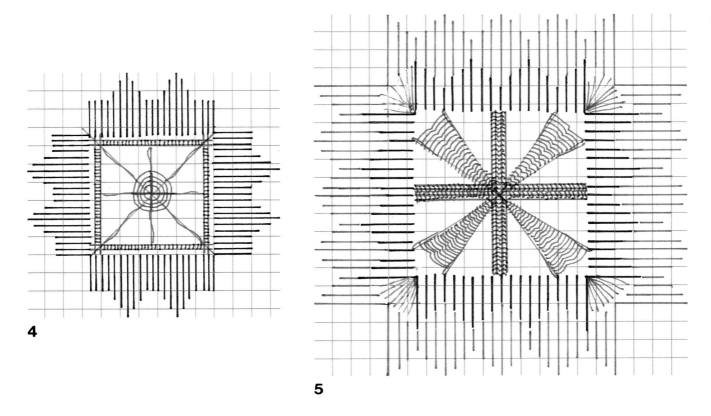

4

5

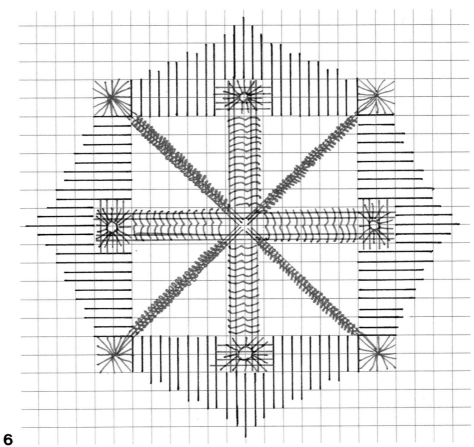

6

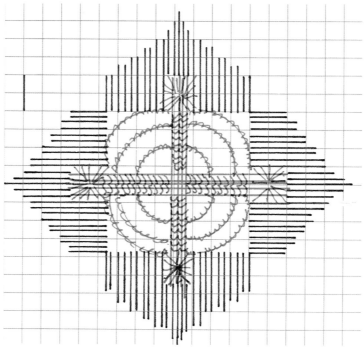

7

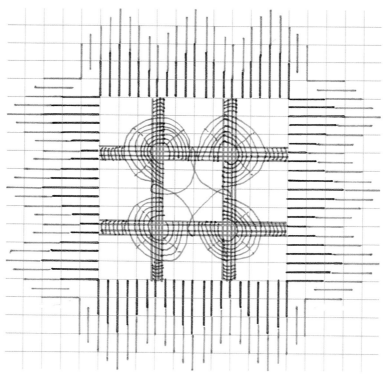

8

Project J

Follows graphs 1 to 8.

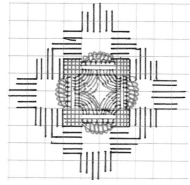

5

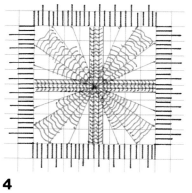

4

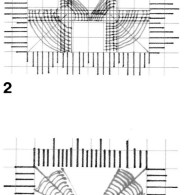

2

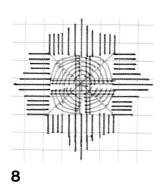

8

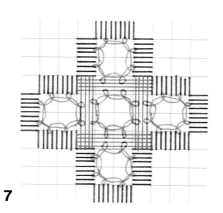

3

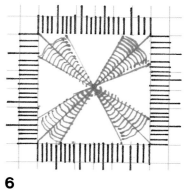

6

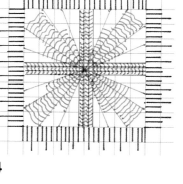

7

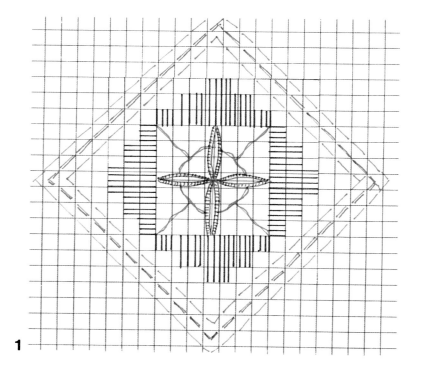

1

Project K

Green fabric, embroidered with brown,
with an unusual centre.

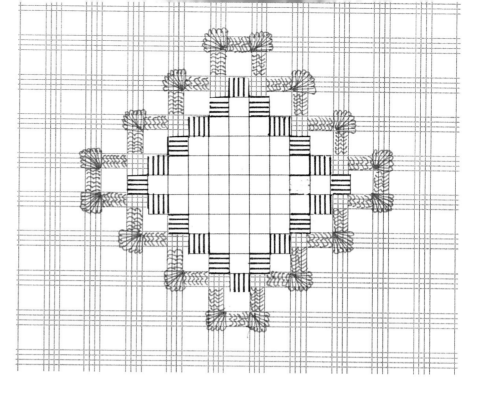

Project L
Blue and white lacy effect.

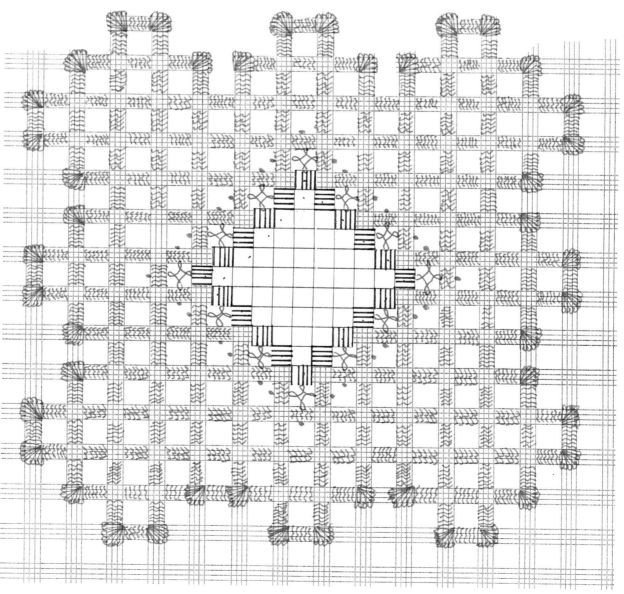

Project M

This shows four different ways of making Maltese Crosses on the outer edging. The inner border is worked with four different ways of needleweaving. Centre has four unusual blocks demonstrating needleweaving as shown in graphs.

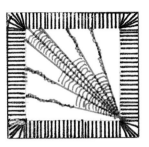
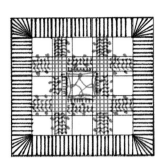

Project N

Soft apricot wall hanging. Inverted Kloster
blocks and needleweaving of spiderweb.

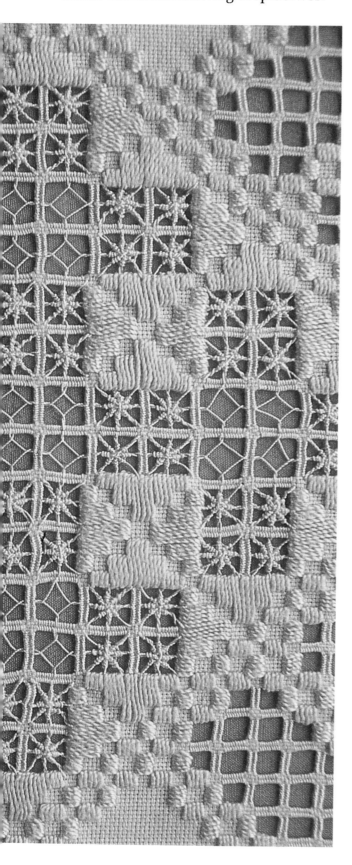

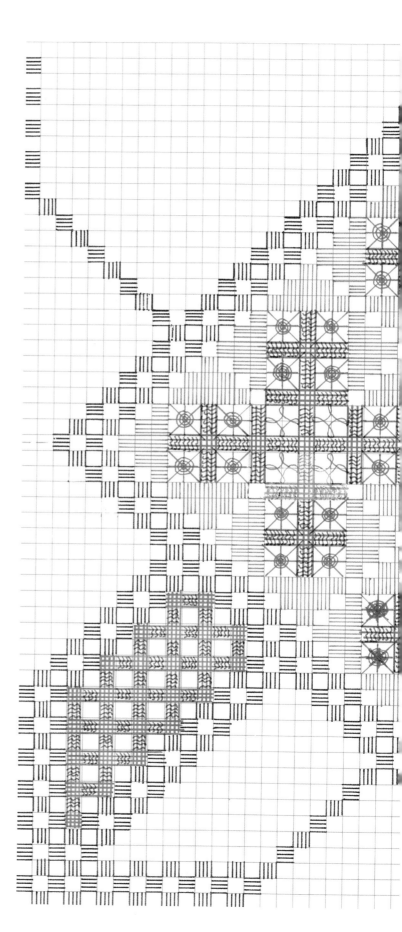

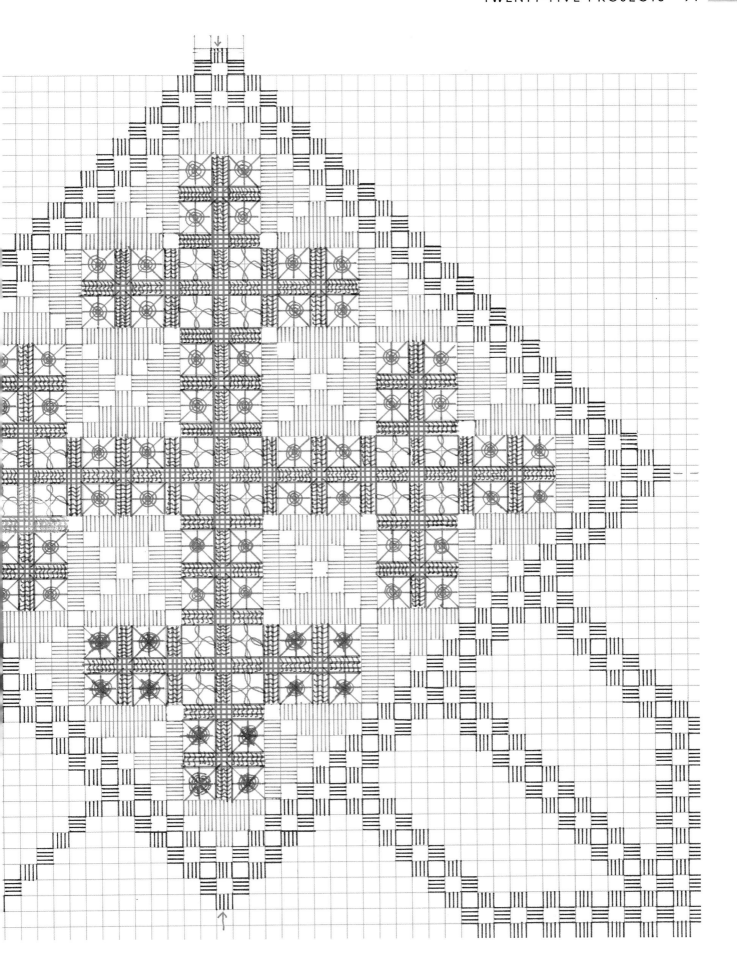

Project O

Worked on brown Lugana illustrating five
different blocks with different needleweaving.

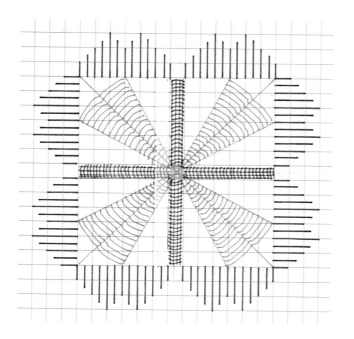

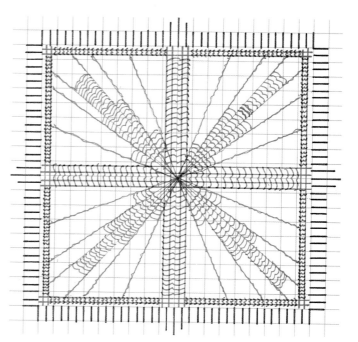

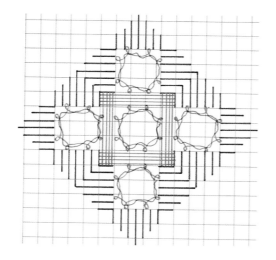

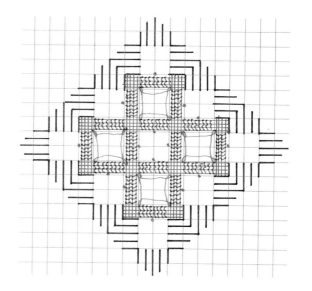

Project P

White table runner worked on Glenshea linen.

See pages 74-75 for detailed graph.

Project Q
See photograph of old rose jacket and skirt.
In the skirt design, note the wide bank of
Hardanger and exquisite border of a
double row of eyelets.
The jacket design is exceptional and
complements the skirt. The design is
an original creation of the author.

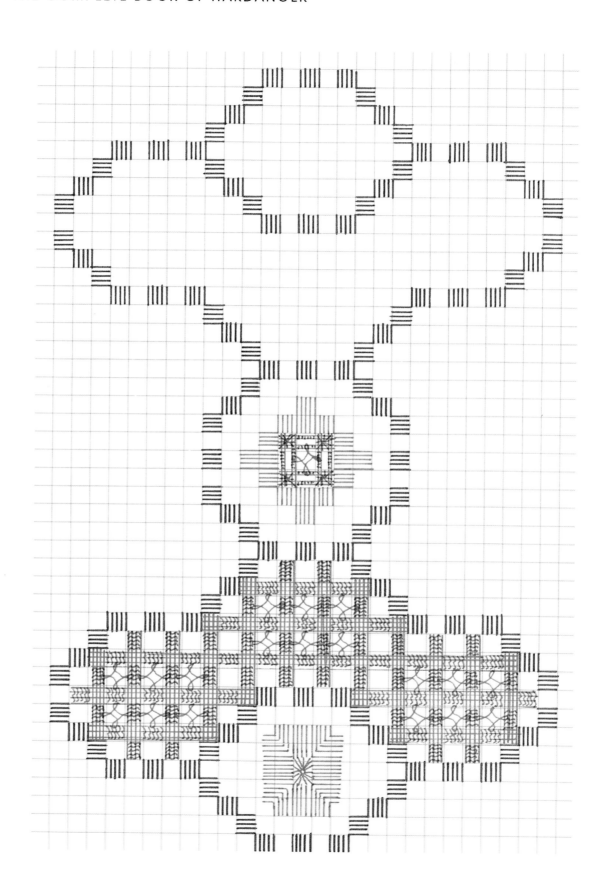

Projects R, S, T, U, V, W

These are examples of other ways in
which Hardanger may be utilised.

Project X

Project Y

Cover design

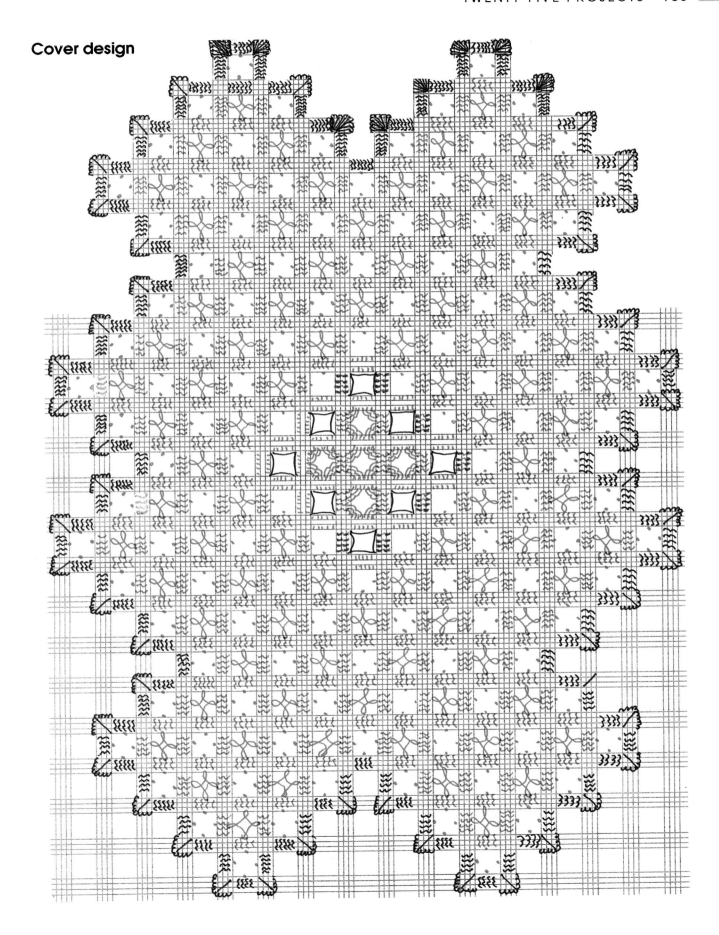

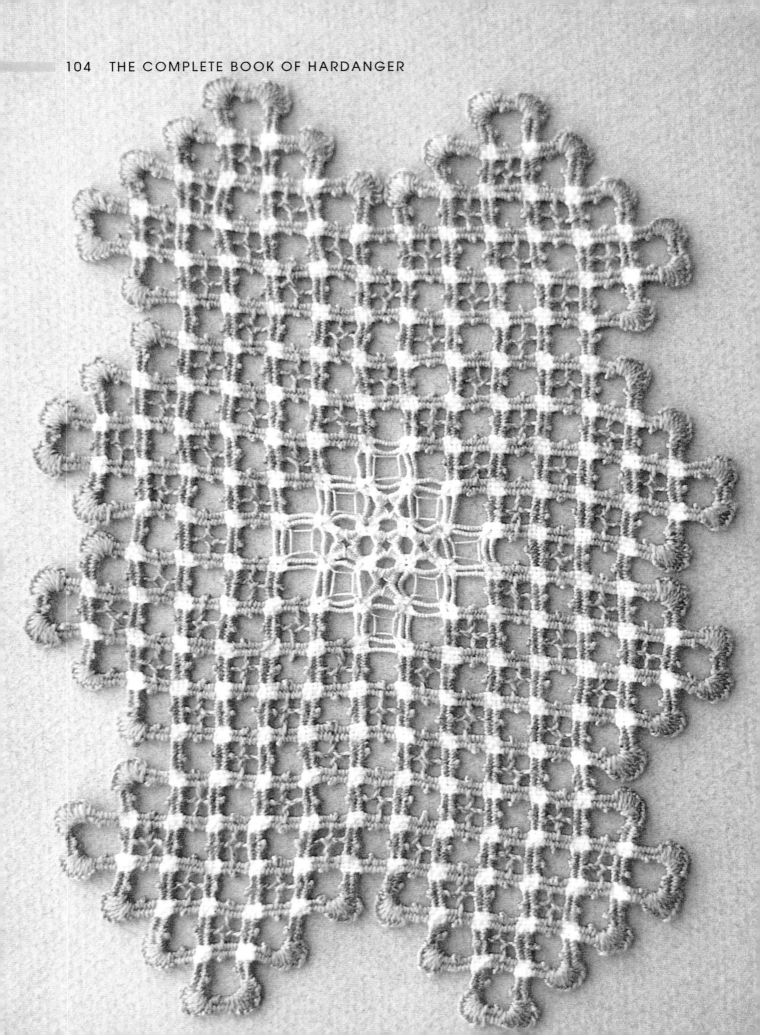

CHAPTER SIX

Finishing the Project

The edge is either buttonholed or hemstitched. If buttonhole stitch is used, cut remaining fabric carefully away from the edge. It is easier to cut from the right side as there is less danger of cutting into the buttonhole stitch. Tidy up at the back and wash softly by hand.

Never iron your embroidery on the right side as the twist of the thread will be flattened. Put a cloth over the wrong side of the embroidery and use medium heat. If lining the work for pillows, pictures, etc, use a darker fabric to show up the design.

Index